# VENTURE TO THE INTERIOR

THE AUTHOR

# VENTURE
# TO THE INTERIOR

by

LAURENS VAN DER POST

THE REPRINT SOCIETY LONDON

FIRST PUBLISHED 1952
THIS EDITION FIRST PUBLISHED BY THE REPRINT SOCIETY LTD.
BY ARRANGEMENT WITH THE HOGARTH PRESS LTD.
1953

*By the same Author*

IN A PROVINCE

THE FACE BESIDE THE FIRE

PRINTED IN GREAT BRITAIN BY RICHARD CLAY AND COMPANY, LTD.,
BUNGAY, SUFFOLK

*I owe a great deal to Frances Cornford, Robert Chapman and my wife, Ingaret Giffard, for helping to prepare the manuscript of this book for publication*

# CONTENTS

# MAPS

# CONTENTS

# PREFACE

ON the morning of May 10, 1949, I sat, full of resentment, at Air Terminal House in London. With me
were about twenty other persons, waiting for a bus to take
us to the aerodrome at Heath Row. I was painfully aware
that once again my life was not proceeding according to
my conscious plan. My bitterness, although it may not have
been excusable, was certainly understandable. Ever since
as a soldier I left England in 1940, I had been longing and
planning to get back, but hitherto the over-all pattern of
my life had shown very little regard either for my planning
or my longing. I was not to see England again between
1940 and 1945.

My own war had taken me further and further away
from England to increasingly unexpected and remote
places, with the prospects of leave at home growing corre-
spondingly less and less. It had led me, with the most
meticulous timing and with an air of predetermined final-
ity, from behind the enemy lines in Abyssinia, from the
Western desert, Syria and the Transjordan frontier,
through the jungles of the Dutch East Indies, to several
years of incarceration in Japanese prisoner-of-war camps.
Then, in August 1945, when the wars of most other soldiers
were coming to an end, mine rediscovered itself and found
in the nationalist resurgence in Java and Sumatra justification for continuing my own private and personal part well
into 1947.

Except for one tantalizing fortnight in October 1945,
when Lord Mountbatten sent me to London to report to
the Prime Minister and the War Cabinet, I did not see
England from 1940 until the August of 1947.

I had come back eagerly then. My prisoner-of-war

conscience was at last at rest. I felt that I had tried to put the sum of the whole above the sum of my own individual part of life, for as long as had been useful or necessary; and perhaps from my own selfish point of view, for even longer than was reasonable or wise.

I had done freely, without any kind of outside compulsion, all that I could to redeem those grim, inarticulate years in prison. For the first time since I had walked into a Japanese trap, nearly five years before, in Java in the valley of Lebaksembada—which, as its Sudanese name nicely implies, was "so well made"—I seemed rid of a certain sense of humiliation. For during those long, seasonless and tranced Indonesian years, I had been dogged by the thought of my friends and countrymen going out daily to battle, while I withered behind prison walls.

I had promised myself then that if I survived, which at that moment seemed most unlikely, I would never again return to a life of nothing but private profit and personal gain. I would try never again to say "NO" to life in its full, complete sense, no matter in how humble or perplexed a guise it presented itself.

From where I was in the midst of it, the war seemed essentially a product of profound negation; the fearful problem child of "NO" parents; of so many generations of such a planned, closely-argued, well-reasoned and determined no-ness, that just saying "NO" to living in its deep, instinctive aspects had become the dreary, unconscious routine. By this wilful, persistent no-ness we had turned one half of life, potentially a rich and powerful ally, into the active and embittered enemy of the other. . . .

One afternoon in 1949 a letter summoned me to an annexe of Whitehall. I was told that in Nyasaland—I always thought of it as the old British Central Africa—there were two tracts of country about which London could not obtain any information it really wanted. One was a huge, rugged mountain mass in the extreme south of the Protectorate; the other a large plateau abruptly and precipitously set from eight to nine thousand feet above the lakes and plains of the extreme north of the territory. Neither, of course, was completely unknown. Both had been partially explored; casually looked at by all kinds of people in the past. Enthusiastic botanists, odd prospectors and hunters, the more enterprising district commissioners, forestry officers and other government officials had all been to these two areas from time to time. They had even been put on the map with a confident air of detailed precision. But now the knowledge that was being gained from flying over them by aeroplane suggested more and more that the maps were misleading, if not spurious, and in any case woefully inadequate.

When all this miscellaneous information was put together here in London it did not amount to much, and was not the sort of knowledge that could be put to any specific use.

Something more definite and up-to-date about these two areas was wanted. And so they asked me if I would go and have a closer look at them on foot, and come back and tell them what they really looked like, not in the days of Livingstone and Tippo Sahib but in this desperate year 1949. And if I was prepared to go, would I go at once, please?

The matter was urgent. Production of food in the world, and particularly in the Empire and Britain, was beginning to fail, in a sort of geometric retrogression, to keep up with increases of population. Moreover, as our troubles with the Argentine so clearly showed, anything that could help to make Britain independent of alien sources of food should be done, and done as quickly as possible. There was a chance that these areas might help.

Put in this way, I hope it is clear from what I have already said that whatever my own wishes, convenience and determination in the matter, I could not have refused to go without doing violence to conscious convictions.

And yet for me, who may well have to face this decision again, the questions inherent in this paradox are not so easily answered. One of the most striking features of the

desperate age in which we live is its genius for finding good
reasons for doing bad things. We, who are its children, can
never be altogether free of this characteristic. Consciously
or unconsciously, we live not only our own individual life
but, whether we like it or not, also the life of our time. We
are our own dark horses. All day long we avow motives
and purposes that are oddly at variance with the things that
we do. For example we have talked more about reason—
we have, on the face of it, loved, honoured and obeyed
reason more in the last century and a half than at any
other epoch, and yet cumulatively and collectively, in the
grand total of all our individual lives, we have produced
more unreason, bigger and fiercer wars, than any other age
in history.

The theme needs no elaboration. I can only say that it
has become almost axiomatic with me to look for a person's
overriding motive, his wider purpose, his deepest plan, in
his achieved results rather than in the eloquent avowals
that he makes to himself and to others. The outer trend
confirms the inner pattern. We all obviously have motives
and forces inside ourselves of which we are stupendously
unaware: I believe that it is the strongest motive, irrespec-
tive of our degree of awareness of it, which produces results.

I am not suggesting that outside influences, the world of
demonstrable fact and circumstance, have no bearing on
the matter, but that is a point of view which has been so
long in favour, and enjoys the patronage of such powerful
and distinguished intellects, that it can well be left to take
care of itself. What needs our understanding and friendship at this restricted moment in time is this other side of
life, so brutally locked out of our awareness that it can only
draw attention to itself indirectly, humbly and secretly in
the joylessness of the results around us. In this nightfall of
the spirit, I have only to look over my shoulder to see this
other side of life coming up over the horizon of our consciousness, like a dark Homeric hull sailing before winds
blowing from the uttermost limits of time.

Plainly, conscious conviction was not the only thing concerned in my case. I could not have spent one half of my life leaving Africa for Europe and the other half returning from Europe to Africa, if it were no more than that.

I would tend to put it down rather to an unresolved conflict between two fundamental elements in my make-up; conscious and unconscious, male and female, masculine and feminine; the continuation of my father and the presence of my mother in me. On one side, under the heading "AFRICA", I would group unconscious, female, feminine, mother; and under "EUROPE" on the other: conscious, male, masculine, father.

## PART I

# THE JOURNEY IN TIME

"We carry with us the wonders
we seek without us: there is all
Africa and her prodigies in us."

SIR THOMAS BROWNE

# Chapter One

AFRICA is my mother's country. I do not know exactly how long my mother's family has lived in Africa; but I do know that Africa was about and within her from the beginning, as it was for me. Her mother, my grandmother, was cradled, if not actually born, in an ox-wagon driving in the thirties of the last century steadfastly deeper into the unknown interior of Southern Africa. The ox-wagon was part of the small and ill-fated Liebenberg Trek. My mother's grandfather was its leader. This little caravan consisting of no more than seven or eight wagons, this small group of people numbering no more than forty or fifty souls, had moved in the far forefront of a vast exodus. They formed part of the great Trek of Dutch farmers from British rule at the Cape.

They had crossed the Karroo safely; hauled their wagons laboriously through the boulder-strewn drifts of the Orange River; crossed the wide, melancholy plains of the Free State and forded the deep, yellow Vaal River. They had gone safely across the highveld of the Transvaal, which was plundered bare and still smoked after the raids of Zulu and Matabele, and were moving into the Bushveld, somewhere near where the town of Louis Trichardt stands to-day, when they in their turn were attacked. We shall never know precisely what happened.

My grandmother was little more than a baby; she could just run about and speak. All that is known about the attack is what was gathered afterwards from the incoherent account in broken Afrikaans given by the half-caste maid, who looked after my grandmother and her baby sister.

According to the maid, the wagons, after a long and exhausting trek, had come to rest the night before on the banks of a fairly big stream. During the night the two little children were very restless and had kept their parents awake with their crying. As a result, the maid was ordered just before dawn to dress the children and take them out of earshot of the wagons. One gets a clear impression from this order of how little the sleeping lager suspected what fate had in store for it. The maid had collected the children and had taken them down to the stream, as she had some washing to do.

She had not been there many minutes when the quiet—that lovely musical, rhythmical quiet of the Bushveld at dawn—was broken with the war-cries and yells of the attacking Kaffirs. She must have walked through a gap in the encircling *impi*[1] just before it drew its horns tight around the sleeping wagons. She snatched the two little girls and, with one under each arm, ran ducking along the side of the stream until she came to a wide, shallow waterfall. The stream fell, as I myself have so often seen them do in Africa, over a wide, overhanging ledge of stone. Behind the water there was a dry hollow, and shelter. The nurse dodged in behind this curtain of water and sat there fearfully all day with her terrified, uncomprehending charges. Late that night she crept out. She found the wagons burnt out and the battered, disfigured bodies of all who had been in them strewn far around.

Somehow, sheltering behind the waterfall by day and going out to forage when it became dark, she kept herself and the children alive. Nearly a week later they were picked up by a party of horsemen, who were wisely patrolling the disturbed country ahead of a much bigger trek following in the Liebenberg tracks.

I have no intention of writing a family history, but this much appeared necessary because it shows, as nothing else

[1] "Impi" is the Zulu or Sindabile for an army or regiment. This force usually attacked in a formation shaped like a crescent moon: thin and light at the tips of the horns; deep and solid in the centre. The task of the horns was to spread out and surround the enemy; that of the centre constantly to reinforce its extreme flanks.

can show, how much Africa is my mother's country. Her mother told her the story repeatedly from as early as she could remember; I heard it similarly from her. I heard it over and over again from my aunts, each telling it with their own slight, colourful variations; but, alas, I never heard it from my grandmother, because she died before I was born. I heard it, however, from my grandfather, who lived to be nearly a hundred.

And he, too, whatever his ancestral origin, was essentially a part of that same Africa. He also, as a young boy, was involved in the great trek to the north; at the age of fourteen and a half he was carrying a man's rifle on his shoulder and was captured by the redoubtable Sir Harry Smith at the battle of Boomplaas in 1848. He fought in the Kaffir and Basuto wars and helped to clear the Free State hills of their last marauding bushmen.

His own farm was called Boesmansfontein, the fountain of bushman. And what a farm it was! I remember, as a child, sitting with him on a hill one Sunday morning, and his pointing out to me how his land stretched as far as we could see in every direction. He had twelve miles of river running through it; a river with a name that suggests an individual and special history of its own: the Knapsack River. His land had long ranges of hills down the centre of it; wide, flower-covered vleis; plains thick with sheep, wild horses, cattle and flickering springbuck.

We were told with an air of implied, delightful and flattering secrecy by my mother that he had bought it all from the Griquas for a couple of barrels of Cape Brandy— red lavender the Griquas called it—and two dozen frock coats and top hats.

My grandfather's house was filled with the strangest, most colourful collection of warm-hearted human relics and harmless scoundrels from the Free State's great and vanishing past. When they became too much for his generous but circumspect spirit, they fled to my mother, whom they had known ever since she was born. In defiance of the cold convention already being thrust on the country by self-conscious patriots from the Cape, who had never risked life and limb in war or trek, they never used the formal "mistress" or even the slightly warmer "Nonna" of the Cape Malays, but insisted on calling her, as her family always did, " The Little Lamb".

There were two little bushmen, for instance, whom my grandfather had brought back with him from the Commando which went to clean up the bands of Jacob Jaer and Pieter Windvoel, the last of the bushmen marauders in the Free State. They were tiny little men, extremely highly strung and at the age of sixty still unashamedly terrified of the dark. But they had a fascinating fund of stories that were religion to them, about animals, insects and worms, about spiders, praying mantises and the moon.

There were also the last lingering strains of the Hottentots, with skins like newly strung telephone wires and haunted Nylotic faces. They too told us endless stories about animals, about wolves, jackals, hares and tortoises, about elephants, birds and baboons, but also about beings half-animal, half-human, and stories of witchcraft and magic under the moon.

Again there were serious, rather business-like Basutos who, under my grandfather's firm hand, carried the real responsibility of working his vast lands. And there were disreputable old Griquas, who knew intuitively that no matter how drunk they became or how often they were jailed for petty theft, they were certain of forgiveness and a sure sustenance, because of my grandfather's conscience. And they knew that they were loved by my mother and her entire family.

There was in particular one old Griqua, Jan Kok, too old for either virtue or sin. He was so old that his age was popularly estimated at anything between one hundred and one hundred and twenty years. But no one, least of all he himself, knew for sure. He was a nephew of Adam Kok, the greatest of the Griqua kings, who had in his day concluded treaties with the British Government. He would sit all day long sunning himself in the kitchen courtyard, and often he would tell me, in a blurred voice, the strangest things about Africa. He told me, for instance, that one part of the Griqua people—the other part, of course, was European—had come from the far northern Interior of Africa, from the other side of mountains which shook and rumbled, sending fire and smoke into the sky.

When his dim old eyes were troubled, he would frequently sing to himself a hymn learnt nearly a hundred years before from the great missionary Dr. Philip, who is hated by so many of my countrymen to this day as though he were still alive. It began: "Lord, how does thy light fall towards the sea," and as he sang I used to think, "Poor old Jan, he has never seen the sea and never will."

After supper in the evenings, all that was human in and about my grandfather's house gathered in the dining-room to listen to him reading from THE BOOK. At those moments there could be seen by the lamplight, lifted attentively to catch some terrible words from the Old Testament, a wrinkled old face of almost every race and colour that had contributed to the history of the country. I have never forgotten the eyes of those Bushmen and Hottentots, on those evenings forty years ago. Those dark eyes that were solemn and glowing with the first light of the world's history; warm and content with the secret of man's earliest days. Some of those races have since vanished for good, and those places that once knew them so well are now only occupied, as though by ghosts, by people of our own colour. And so I could continue for a long time, but these fragments must suffice to suggest how it was at the beginning.

One final word about my mother. At the age of seventy she suddenly distressed her children, grandchildren and her vast circle of friends and acquaintances by refusing, in the most resolute and absolute fashion, to live peacefully, quietly and comfortably in civilized surroundings. Instead, she installed herself, with a European maid, on one of her largest farms which had deteriorated under hired management. It proved too lonely and rough a life for the maid, who soon left. My mother, however, continued for some years alone with her Basuto servants, until the property was completely rehabilitated and once more pleasing to her fastidious eye. Her children then hoped that she would have had enough, and tried to persuade her to come and live in comfort, where they could see and visit her regularly. But she refused, for she had only ended the first stage of another life.

She moved on to an even more remote and backward farm. In due course that too was restored to the semblance of a well-cared-for establishment and my mother promptly gave it to a son who had just come back from the war in Italy. Then, before the old argument could again be raised by her children, she went even farther away.

Many years ago my father had bought a vast tract of land on the edge of the Kalahari desert. For fifty years no one had made any effort to develop it, and those broad acres were left there, lying parched and unwanted in the desert sun. There my mother went at the age of eighty. The only people who seemed willing to accompany her were displaced persons; there was a German geologist who had been interned during the war; a delicate Bavarian missionary, whom she had made her secretary; and an Italian carpenter and mason, an ex-prisoner of war, who became her foreman.

A hundred miles from the nearest village, they pitched their tents and started looking for water, without which no permanent settlement was possible. At first they hired from private contractors the machines to drill for the water. The German geologist's knowledge of his science and my mother's intuitive assessment between them determined where the drilling should take place. The first contractor drilled down to 150 feet, struck iron stone—or so he said—and refused to continue.

There was a terrible scene out there in the desert between the determined old lady who refused to change the site of the contractor's task, for she was convinced that water was there, and the cynical technician whose profits, if any, decreased the deeper he drilled. In the end the contractor departed.

A second contractor, drilling a few feet away from the first hole, after going down 147 feet, lost all his tackle in the shaft and moved away in disgust. A third contractor, drilling still in the same narrow area, found after 153 feet that he had sunk his shaft at an angle, and could not continue. He too went, bitter and deeply out-of-pocket. By this time no new contractor could be tempted to try his fortune at this notorious site. There was nothing for it but for my mother to buy her own drilling machine. The aged geologist was apprenticed for some months to one of the few remaining unestranged drilling contractors in the area, in order to acquire this new craft; then drilling was resumed in earnest.

Nearly three years had gone by out there in the Kalahari desert, with the burning suns of its summer, and the searing, cold winds of its winter. One of the worst droughts in memory, bringing great storms of dust and sand, broke over them. But the party continued confidently.

Every morning at six my mother rang a hand-bell and handed her employees steaming bowls of coffee that she had made herself. "Men are like that," she says; "they are like children who will get out of bed for food if for nothing else."

Having thus enticed them out of bed, she set them drilling. At 157 feet, only four feet deeper than the deepest shaft sunk by a contractor, they struck water.

"It was most dramatic," my mother said. "I was watching the machine at that moment quite by chance"—of course, her eyes never left it—"when suddenly I saw it lurch slightly. All the slack in the rope of the drill disappeared. The bore was through the stone and in a deep vein of water. It came gushing up the shaft."

So sure had she been all along that water would be found, that the pumps were there waiting; they had been waiting for three years ready to go up the moment that water was found.

There my mother is to this day, a slim, lovely, upright, gracious old lady, whose skin looks as if it has never known anything but European sun. She is still active, vigorous, young in spirit and convinced that she will live to be a hundred and twenty. She builds, plants trees and orchards, and grows corn in a desert where neither corn nor grass grew before.

We, her children, have all been bitterly reproached by close friends and well-meaning relations for letting her live in this way. Frankly I have not even the excuse that the others have, for they have done their best to dissuade her, whereas I have actively and whole-heartedly encouraged her. She seems to me happier now than she has ever been, in spite of the difficulties, anxieties and extreme discomforts of this new way of life.

It has often occurred to me that the heavy burden of bearing and rearing children—and my mother reared thirteen—has, in a sense, been irrelevant to the deepest and most vital purpose of her life. I have never been able to believe that a woman's task in life is limited to her children. I can quite well conceive that in my mother, as with more and more women of our own day, there is an urge to creativeness which lies underneath and deeper, above and beyond the begetting of children. These women have a contract with life itself, which is not discharged by the mere procreation of their species. Men recognize and try to honour this contract in themselves as a matter of course. Their contribution to life vibrates with their passionate rebellion against the narrowly conceived idea that would restrict their role to that of protectors and feeders of women and children. They do not acknowledge and respect the same thing so readily in women. Perhaps until they do the world will not see the full creative relationship that life intends there should be between men and women.

As far as my mother is concerned, I was moved and reassured by this development so late in her life. For me her story is a source of unfailing confidence in the future. After many years in which the need to create must have been consciously forgotten, overlaid by a thousand anxieties of birth and death, war and peace, when it should, by all the dictates of reason, have vanished for good, then suddenly as an old lady my mother was able to turn round and find the same urge close beside her, throwing, in the gathering darkness round her feet, the clear, familiar light she had known as a child. For this it is that mother has done, and I would like it to be told as a memorial of her. After sixty uninterrupted years as a wife and a mother she turned confidently to the authentic and original vision of her life, and was at once enabled to pursue the dream of her African girlhood.

# Chapter Two

How different was my father's background and beginning. Again, I promise not to go into a detailed history of my family; I will keep only to a few selected facts, which may possibly help to define this most difficult and intangible dimension of my African journey.

My father was born in Holland; he was of Europe as even my mother could never be of Africa. For, far back, something of Europe must have gone into the making of my mother's family, but there were no known un-European elements even in my father's remotest beginnings. He was the eldest member of a family which had its roots deep in the life and, to a not undistinguished extent, in the history of the country. One ancestor, for instance, as far back as 1572, had played a noble role when Leyden was desperately besieged by the forces of the grim Duke of Alva. Since then representatives of the family have kept on appearing and reappearing at all kinds of dramatic moments in the history of the Netherlands; here on a battlefield; there following the House of Orange to exile in Britain; now at Quatre-Bras refusing a royal command to withdraw, because of a half-shot-away arm, with a "God, sire, damnation to the thought while I have the other"; then leading an expedition to the Indies; and so on. No one action perhaps important enough to justify inclusion in text-books, but more than enough to bring a warm glow into the cold archives and legends of the family.

Unfortunately, I knew my father's parents only from their portraits. One of the major disadvantages of being a thirteenth child is that one appears on the family stage when so much that is old, interesting and traditional in its trappings has either changed irrevocably for the worse, or disappeared for good. So many of the principal actors have by then spoken their piece, and gone home. Both my grandparents were dead by the time I was born, but my grandmother in her pictures looks a most lovely, slim, elegant woman, with fearless, warm, inexhaustible eyes.

She was not Dutch, but came of a French family distinguished for its devotion to music and the arts. According to my mother, my grandmother herself sang beautifully, and her voice was greatly favoured at the Court of Holland, where, judging by the notes in her music books, she sang on many intimate occasions. I myself have fingered her music books, carefully and lovingly preserved, and, as a child, tried to play from the yellowing score that she had transcribed in her clear, fastidious hand.

About her husband, my grandfather, there had always seemed to me to be a conspiracy of silence in the family. People would talk about my grandmother with a warm, infectious enthusiasm, as if the recollection of her gave them joy. But at the mention of my grandfather they became either completely silent or very evasive. I have not to this day heard the true story.

It appears that some disgrace, some shattering financial disaster was connected with him. I do not know what it was, but, very far back, very near the conscious beginning, I seem to remember my father saying to someone: "It was not his fault really; it would not have happened if he had not guaranteed the debts of his greatest friend."

But I know that just over half-way through the last century my father's family suddenly uprooted itself, and disappeared from Holland for good. Just about a century ago my grandfather, profoundly embittered, dropping a title and half the name of the family on the way, arrived suddenly with his wife and three children in South Africa. So foreign was Africa to them, so outside their experience and imagination, so unforeseen, that when a husky negro at Capetown came wading out to their boat to carry them ashore my grandmother is reported to have cried out with dismay: "Oh, Bill, please do not surrender the children to the devil."

The burden of this unforeseen and precipitate migration fell heavily on my father. Looking back on it, and making full allowance for the fact that I was not there, I think he was extremely gallant about it; and I feel that his life would have been easier if there had been people with him who could have appreciated this and told him how brave he was being.

He resolutely put behind him all that there had been of promise and expectation in Europe, and at an early age started to be the main support of his family.

His only asset was his European background, with its culture and education. He went into the remote interior, and hired himself out as a teacher to the children of the Trekker Boers. They, like my South African countrymen to this day, had a respect and hunger for education that must be experienced to be fully believed.

His first employment as a teacher brought him his keep and a pound a month. He asked for his first payment to be made in silver, not only because it had to be carefully distributed to his family, but also because, like that, it would seem much more. For a time he taught children of all ages and sizes, from far and near in the Southern Free State. Amongst these was my mother, a sturdy little girl of seven, who, day after day, solemnly and somewhat hypnotized, stared at him out of large grey eyes which were nearly hidden under a thick crown of rich brown hair.

All this time he was teaching himself the law of the New Republic; and in due course he qualified as a barrister. In time he had the largest legal practice in the Free State. He threw himself with great determination into the work and life around him, driven I suspect far more by will than by instinctive enthusiasm. He took part in everything outside his profession; in farming, mining and building railways; in opening-up new country; and in politics. At one time he was well in the running for the presidency of the

Free State. He would have got it, I think, if the people had not found something foreign in him.

Hollanders—cheese-heads as they are disdainfully called to this day in South Africa—were not popular in the Republic. Anyway, my father never became President, but at the outbreak of the Boer War he was chairman of the Executive Council of the Old Free State Parliament. For two years he was out on Commando. My mother's only brother was killed at his side. On one occasion he slipped through the advancing British lines, and went far back into the hills of the Southern Free State in a vain effort to rally the discouraged burghers, who were flocking home in their hundreds. For months, abandoned by everyone except a kinsman of my mother, he slept out in bushveld and on hilltops, with enemy fires by night and enemy patrols by day round him, separating him from his own armed forces, rather as I did for some years, in this last war, with Italians in Abyssinia, and Japanese in Java. About eight months before the end, whilst Commandant of Barberton, he was caught by General French. He was the second prisoner-of-war in my family; I was the third.

When Vereeniging came, my father refused to take the oath of allegiance, and consequently was refused permission by the British authorities to return to the Free State. For the first time in his life he felt consciously and profoundly bitter. He was a generous, chivalrous and essentially a fair person. Not just the defeat of the Republic, but the actual fact that there could have been such a war, was a profound shock to him. He was present at that fatal meeting between Lord Milner and Kruger in Bloemfontein in 1899. He was one of the few people there who knew English and Englishmen well; he admired them, and had a host of English friends. But he came back from that meeting with a clear conviction that no matter what concessions were made, Milner would have his war.

For four years he refused to alter his decision not to become a British subject. He and his family were confined to

Stellenbosch in the Cape. In those four years he wrote two
novels about South Africa's itinerant past. He wrote them
partly in Dutch and partly in Afrikaans, which was still an
unrecognized, unwritten, apologetically spoken language.
Then came Campbell-Bannerman's great gesture. My
father's bitterness left him. He discovered then in his heart
not only forgiveness, but also a living, constructive appre-
ciation of something magnanimous. He packed up at once,
returned to the Free State, and worked heart and soul for
the Union that came in 1910.

It has always been to me one of the more frightening
ironies of Afrikaner life that people like my father, who
with Smuts and Botha had actually fought and suffered in
the war, could forgive and begin anew, whereas others,
alive to-day, who were never in the heart of that conflict,
can still find it so hard to forgive an injury that was not
even done to them. And how can there ever be any real
beginning without forgiveness?

I noticed something similar in my own experience when
I met War Crimes officers, who had neither suffered intern-
ment under the Japanese nor even fought against them.
They were more revengeful and bitter about our treatment
and our suffering in prison than we were ourselves.

I have so often noticed that the suffering which is most
difficult, if not impossible, to forgive is unreal, imagined
suffering. There is no power on earth like imagination,
and the worst, most obstinate grievances are imagined
ones. Let us recognize that there are people and nations
who create, with a submerged deliberation, a sense of
suffering and of grievance, which enable them to evade
those aspects of reality that do not minister to their self-
importance, personal pride or convenience. These imagined ills enable them to avoid the proper burden that life
lays on all of us.

Persons who have really suffered at the hands of others
do not find it difficult to forgive, nor even to understand
the people who caused their suffering. They do not find it

difficult to forgive because out of suffering and sorrow truly endured comes an instinctive sense of privilege. Recognition of the creative truth comes in a flash: forgiveness for others, as for ourselves, for we too know not what we do.

This perpetuation of so-called "historic" and class grievances is an evil, dishonest and unreal thing. It is something which cannot be described adequately in the customary economic, political and historical clichés. The language that seems far more appropriate is the language of a pathologist describing cancer, the language of a psychologist describing a deep-seated complex and obsessional neurosis. For what is Nazism, or present-day Malanism in this Southern Africa of my youth, but the destruction of the whole by an unnatural proliferation of the cells of a part, or a wilful autonomous system that would twist the whole being to a partial need?

I have gone into this aspect at some length because no one to-day can let his mind dwell on the Africa which is moving darkly and secretly to fulfilment, without becoming aware of this diabolic absence of good.

It is even more relevant to the immediate story that my father himself could never understand or reconcile himself to this fundamental South African irony. And when finally it reared its head again obstinately and fanatically in the significant Hertzog–Botha and Smuts breach, he withdrew altogether from politics, from public affairs and even from his own profession, and retired to his many thousands of acres of land.

It is in this short period that I have my clearest recollection of him. It is a portrait of someone finally recognizing himself as alien to the life and country about him; of someone whose nerves were frayed almost to breaking-point by the world about him. Everything in his town house and in the numerous farms where he stayed from time to time, suggested then an instinctive rejection of Africa, and a reaffirmation of Europe.

The walls were covered with old Dutch oil-paintings; the carpets and furniture were Dutch, and the long corridor of the large house in town was laid out with cool, black and gold tiles, specially imported from Holland.

Even the food we ate was curiously un-African. Once a month a large case containing cheeses like full moons, preserved fish, tinned hams, Chinese ginger in Delft jars and rare delicacies came to us from a merchant in Holland, who knew my father's numerous brood by name, and from time to time included some tasty surprise for one or another of them.

To our horses on the farms, to the cattle and the pet cows, to the sheep, dogs, cats and numerous tame animals of all kinds which he allowed to wander freely round the houses and, in the early mornings, even in the bedrooms of the children, he gave the most resounding names taken from the history of the Netherlands. I had two pet lambs who answered to the names of Hoorn and Egmont, and who were permitted to make spirited overtures to me while still in bed. There were two superb, prancing golden stallions, specially imported from Gelderland, they glorying in the names of Gouda and Treslong, the Lords of Holland who led the Beggars of the Sea against Philip's Spanish galleons. These stallions his eldest sons and one daughter mounted and fell from with gallant and desperate regularity.

His library, where he spent much of the day, was filled with a most comprehensive and unusual collection of European literature, in five languages. In the centre of his desk always stood a mortar and pestle made from the muzzle of a gun captured from the Spaniards by his favourite ancestor. At one side was a large cabinet filled, appropriately, with a remarkable selection of rare and ancient European coins; the currency of his spirit was obviously not there, then and of that moment.

In those last years a tremendous warmth, tenderness and love went out from him to everything round about him, as if to balance the growing estrangement with the outside world. In retrospect there seems to me to have been a deep, valedictory quality about it; an inarticulate foreknowledge that his day was drawing to a close. But into all his relationships of those years and into the life about him he seemed to pour an unfailing stream of kindliness, of generosity and love. It excluded nothing; the trees, the flowers in the large garden, the servants and employees, the contractors and shopkeepers, the animals, the dogs, the pet monkeys, the tame lynxes and jackals and birds; all shared in it. Early every morning he was out in the garden, and would himself call his daughters with a flower freshly picked for each and his sons with a peach, pear, fig or bunch of grapes. No man, beast or animal called on him in vain for help. He wore his heart on his sleeve. The lame dogs from miles around flocked about him. A little one-legged African wagtail came regularly into his study in the mornings to be fed. His children, when they speak of him as he was at this period, betray the quality of the man in the warm animation that breaks into their voices.

But I know he was profoundly unhappy. I remember one night being snatched out of bed and being made to hold him round his knees and plead with him not to go out and kill someone. I do not know precisely what was the trouble, but he stood there shaking with rage, his sword in his hand. He would sit for hours playing melancholy tunes to himself on an ancient concertina, or humming to himself his old Commando hymn: "Rough storms may rage, around me all is night. But God my God will not forsake me."

How could one, at the age of seven, have known what it was all about? How could one have known that it was not possible to understand and return, as it should have been returned, this tremendous outpouring of tenderness and affection in that place, at that time and in those circumstances; that love is

B

> "*The unfamiliar name*
> *Behind the hands that wove*
> *The intolerable shirt of flame,*
> *Which human power cannot remove.*"

Finally, how could any of us, who had not shared his beginnings, have known that, night and day, his blood murmured its own sense of his exile like a far sea in his ears? He died in 1914 within a few days of the outbreak of war. When it happened it seemed to me as if the walls of a warm, brightly lit room, in which I had been sitting, had suddenly collapsed, allowing the night from beyond the farthest range of stars to come rushing in.

The doctors said he died of double pneumonia. I know he died of exile.

There was not a part of my being to which that knowledge did not penetrate in the years that followed, and with it a growing realization that somehow my life must find a way out between my father's exile and my mother's home. It was as if far back at its source, long before birth, life had divided into two deep streams flowing on parallel courses that could not meet this side of infinity. It presupposed, in its ultimate meaning, this among other journeys.

## PART II

# THE JOURNEY THROUGH SPACE

*"Notre vie est un voyage*
*Dans l'Hiver et dans la Nuit,*
*Nous cherchons notre passage*
*Dans le Ciel où rien ne luit."*

**OLD SWISS SONG**

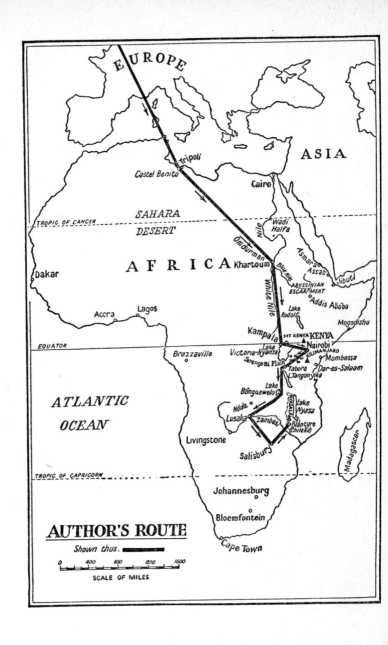

EUROPE

ASIA

Tripoli
Castel Benito
Cairo

TROPIC OF CANCER
SAHARA
DESERT

AFRICA

Nile
Wadi
Halfa

Omdurman
Khartoum
Blue Nile
Asmara
Assab

White Nile

Dakar

ABYSSINIAN
ESCARPMENT
Addis Ababa
Djibuti

Accra
Lagos

Lake
Rudolf

Mogadishu

EQUATOR

Kampala
MT KENYA KENYA
Nairobi

Brazzaville

Lake
Victoria-Nyanza
Serengetti Plain
KILIMANJARO
Mombassa
Dar-es-Salaam

Tabora
L. Tanganyika

ATLANTIC

Lake
Banguewelo

Lake
Nyasa

OCEAN

Ndda
Lusaka
Zambesi
Blantyre
(Chileka)

Livingstone

Salisbury

Madagascar

TROPIC OF CAPRICORN

Johannesburg

Bloemfontein

# AUTHOR'S ROUTE

*Shown thus.* ▬▬▬

0    400   800   1200   1600

SCALE OF MILES

Cape Town

# Chapter Three

I AM by now aware that I have talked almost exclusively about the mental load I was taking with me on my journey. I have said nothing, though it is traditional on these occasions, about what I had packed in my suitcases. The truth is that the journey might well have proved incomprehensible without some account of the state of mind and feelings that I brought to it, whereas the load in my suitcases was light and of little interest.

I do not know how the average traveller to the more remote parts of Africa equips himself nowadays for the journey. He used to do fantastic things before the war, and probably still does. I have always bought as little and made as few arrangements in advance as possible.

For instance, I had not ordered special boots, shoes or leggings. Nor was I tempted to buy any Stanley–Livingstone headgear, green and white pagodas (topees with sun-flaps lined with red flannel), having for years suspected the designers of these things of being bald persons determined to promote baldness in others. The tropical sun is kinder to European heads than they perhaps deserve, and I myself do not find it necessary to wear anything more in Africa than I would for the midsummer sun of Europe.

I had no preconceived theory about the kind of rifle I should take with me. I knew all about the famous pre-war controversy over rifles: the merits and demerits of the .22, the light high-velocity sporting make, the .375 magnum express, the Paradox, and the heavy elephant gun. I did not waste a thought as to whether one or a combination of two or more of these would best serve my particular purpose. I ordered no special supplies of food, ammunition or medicine. I felt as if I already had inside me all the medicine that I could ever need, as a result of the absurd and ever-growing number of injections inflicted on air travellers.

It has always been a source of wonder to me what the trader, be he Jew, Greek, Indian or lonely Scot, can produce from behind the counter of his galvanized-iron store, even in the most out-of-the-way parts of Africa. I have an immense respect too for the experience and opinions in these matters of the men on the spot. In a continent as vast as Africa the needs of an individual vary enormously according to locality, and I have found that it pays well to shop, prepare, organize and seek advice as near as possible to the starting-point of my journey.

So all I did was to add to my store of khaki clothing, to choose some books for the journey, because they can be difficult to find in Africa, and to lay in a small supply of sealing-wax. I was doubtful whether I could get sealing-wax at my destination, and I could not risk being without it as I needed it for making secure the samples I hoped to collect on my journey. But all in all, I was taking so little that my friends, with their warm and affectionate concern for what is individual and eccentric, quickly created a legend among themselves. Would one believe it, they said, that I had gone off again to Central Africa with a stick of scarlet sealing-wax in one hand and a copy of George Meredith's *Modern Love* in the other?

Broadly speaking, it was in this mood and in this manner that the journey began for me. On May 10 at noon precisely our plane took off from Heath Row aerodrome. It is a measure of the newness which still infects air travel that, although once in the air it completes a journey between two points with the utmost dispatch, at the same time it condemns travellers to dreary hours of waiting and preparation on the ground; to tiresome formalities with Customs, Exchange and Immigration controls at all kinds of places, and finally to cumbersome and ponderous journeys by road to and from aerodromes. It took us two hours, after leaving Victoria, to get into the air. But once in the air, no one could have had any complaints over the speed at which we travelled.

I do not know what my twenty companions were thinking as we took off, but once again I was struck by the brutal, impersonal quality of this form of departure. I have never ceased to be touched in some indefinable way by a ship casting off and moving out to sea. There is something symbolic about it to which the hungry, starved rationalism of our twentieth-century mind instantly and inevitably responds. The ship is of the authentic, antique material of the imagination. It must be impossible for a person of average sensitiveness to say good-bye to someone he loves who is going away in a ship, without experiencing, whether he likes it or not, something of the truth of the trite, but none-the-less pointed French proverb "*Partir c'est mourir un peu*". Even at a railway station, the flutter of a handkerchief, the wave of a hand or a face looking back at one from a window, to some extent redeems the train's impersonal yet hysterical departure. The aeroplane makes none of these concessions. There is no interval between the "being here" and the "going there"; the two conditions are created, as it were, with one stroke of the knife, and one is left with a vague, uncomprehended sense of shock. One feels as if one had been subjected to a lightning amputation.

At one moment we were in England in the spring, and at the next we were above it in seasonless and indeterminate air. We climbed quickly. One familiar landmark after another slid into view with a certain irrevocable ease and then floated out of sight behind us. We had not been up many minutes when I noticed with dismay that we were already coming over the South Downs. It was not until that moment that I realized fully the enormity of the accomplished break.

Only a few days before, on the Saturday and Sunday, I

had walked with a friend through those fields and beside those hedges. It had been my first taste of spring for ten years. I now looked at my diary and saw the drawing I had made that Sunday of a cart-horse grazing in a field, with the long line of the downs behind, a fluff of cloud above, and the spit of a modest, stone-tiled spire topped by a crooked weathervane. And I remembered that while I was sketching, the air was so charged with sunlight, with invisible essences and the steady rhythmical movement of trees, so filled with the scent of flowers and fields in bloom, that the bees appeared not to fly through the air but to swim in it. For there is no spring, as Europe knows it, anywhere in Africa or the tropical east. There is never a comparable process of such complete, utter and uncompromising renewal of every detail of natural life. Well, we might be over that world now, but we were no longer of it.

Some children began to play in the plane. There was a little girl with the old-young face of the European child in Africa. Over her shoulder was slung a leopard-skin bag, and I could tell almost for sure at which shop in Nairobi she had bought it. There was a little boy wearing the colours of a well-known preparatory school in Southern Rhodesia, already a little white master of everything except himself. And there were the parents with the strained, set, official faces that one knows from experience will only become warm and smiling, in Africa, with sunset and the sundowner.

The man in front of me was a plumber from Birmingham. He had heard that the mines in Johannesburg were short of plumbers, so he had taken a few weeks off, at his own expense, to look at conditions. If he liked it, he would settle in South Africa for good. Despite all the money he made, he did not like post-war Britain; "too cramped," he said, "too many restrictions". I thought to myself: "There he is, the Pilgrim Father, 1949 model, complete with motive."

There was a young surveyor still wearing Varsity

flannels and a brown tweed coat, pleased and thrilled to
be on his way to work for the Colonial Survey Department
in the neighbourhood of Tabora. There was a business
man from Tanganyika; strangely, he looked more like a
certain general, under whom I had served, than the
general did himself.

There was a Director of Agriculture, a nice man with a
record of devoted service, but already assuming, with a
certain relief, one suspected, some of the importance that
would automatically descend on him at his destination.
There were some other officials returning from leave; an
Army sister on her way to Eritrea; a missionary and his
wife on the way back to Uganda; and two commercial
travellers, in the grand manner, dressed just a little too
well for the occasion.

The plane itself was being flown by a South African
crew. It was a well-known, popular, much-advertised
American model, which I personally rather dislike. It is
fast and reliable, and technically, I am sure, a very good
machine. But it is designed, like so many American aircraft, with only one aim: to hurl through the air, as fast as
possible, the maximum number of people. I longed for the
slower, more comfortable, British flying-boats with their
obstinate, old-fashioned respect for privacy and individual
needs.

By the time lunch was served we were high over Paris.
The lunch dealt another blow to the memory of Europe.
Everything—the meat, the fruit, the salads—was South
African, with the sharp, almost metallic tang of the typical
Southern African product. The people who served it had
an equivalent tang in their voices; as I looked at them I
suddenly realized that the world of modern travel is very
small. Living in London or Paris, unless one plans carefully, it is difficult to see enough of one's friends. But on
the highways and skyways of the world one meets and re-
meets the same faces. Even I recognized several of the
crew with whom I had travelled before.

I was not surprised, therefore, when the captain of the aircraft, as he came down the plane towards me, looked like someone I had seen before. But I was startled a minute later when he stopped by me and said laughingly, "You don't still think I am a German?"

I recognized him instantly. His name was Jakobus Gerhardus van Waveren. He had been to school with me, was three years my junior and came of an old Free State family. As a pilot he had come to my rescue once during the war in Abyssinia. It is like that with the war. One thinks one has forgotten about it, and then a certain look on the face of a stranger one passes in the street, the sunlight on a broken wall, the distant sound of blasting in the hills, the village butcher shooting a pig in his backyard, the smell of rubber in the rain, a bar of music at nightfall, and there is the war back at once, fresh and alive, deeply embedded in naked senses. The violence with which the memory assails one is always startling. How clearly I remembered this occasion!

Nine years before, Jakobus Gerhardus's plane had flown out of the blue sky one afternoon, circling round our first landing-strip in the Gojjam. He flew a three-engined machine with corrugated wings. At that time the only plane I knew shaped like that was the German Junkers bomber. I remembered being dismayed, thinking "Are we now going to have real Prussian precision bombing on top of everything?"—and I nearly ordered my men to open fire with all we had. But the plane's apparent friendliness and its determination to land held me back. None the less, we kept it covered until I saw, in that crystal-blue, nostalgic light of the Abyssinian mountains, men in South African uniform step out of it. So near had I been to shooting, so overcome was I by the narrowness of my escape, that I had greeted Jakobus Gerhardus ungraciously, saying something like: "How the hell do you expect people not to take you for a German if you fly about in a thing like that?"

He had taken it kindly and replied: "Never you mind. Come and see what I've got for you. "

From that day onwards, all of us who were with Dan Sandford and Orde Wingate had had an assured source of supply from the air. Our long and precarious supply line depending on camels whose route one could have followed blindfold for hundreds of miles, going only by the stink of dead animals, could at last be closed.

"I hardly thought it could be you," Jakobus Gerhardus now said, "when I saw your name on the passenger list. I thought the Japanese did for you. I read your obituary notices in the papers years ago. Are you going home? What do you think of my new kite?"

I was tremendously pleased to see him, and I enjoyed to the full this moment of being with someone whom I had known when I was young. He had a rich fund of information, about persons whom I had not seen for years. But talking of our past in Africa, when I said "I would rather like to go back there for a bit", he hesitated and then remarked, "I don't think you would, much."

"Why not?" I asked, surprised.

He answered at length. Things had changed a lot. Many of our old friends had gone; many of the older families had moved out. A lot of people had come from the South, from the Cape, "R-rolling bolanders", to take their place. "Paarl, Wellington and Dal Josafat run the show now," he said. "A bunch of fanatics, you know. Politics is a dirty game." Then he hastened to add loyally, "I am sure our Union politics are no worse than other people's. But when you think how we whites quarrel among ourselves, with all those blacks about, and the Communists . . ." He paused and then told me that John had become a Communist, had adopted a black baby and was bringing it up in the same nursery with his own white child.

I was deeply interested. John was a school friend. His grandfather had served with my father on the Free State

Council, and accompanied Botha and Smuts on their great mission to Britain. "But why a Communist?" I asked.

"He says that it's the only honest solution to our problems. But, God, Communism is going very, very, very far. As for adopting a black son, God, it is going much too far. We can't stand for that. It just can't be done. My God, you know that."

He looked at me, obviously troubled, and added: "And yet you know old John has always been one of the best. I don't understand what's bitten him." He then jumped up suddenly and said: "Come and look at my kite!"

I would have liked to ask more about John but I dared not. I followed him silently into the cockpit.

We were well over France. Grenoble was just coming up under the starboard wing. The air was blue, cool and clear. Suddenly the peak of Mont Blanc, not white but a deep golden colour, came out of the haze of the horizon. It lifted its head like the muzzle of a great polar bear sniffing the air for news of ice.

"Seldom see it like that!" the pilot shouted in my ear. "It's obviously your lucky day." But it was really his luck and his pleasure, and my irony.

The river Isère, blue and silver, flashed the sun back at us from the ground. Just outside the town of Grenoble, I could see plainly La Ponatière, a house of which I had many happy memories. It stood out formal and flat like an architect's drawing of itself, with the trees of the avenue that runs from the gates up to the house looking more like shrubs in pots than the plane trees they really are.

"Look, the Alps!" he called again. And there they were far to the east, a remote vision of snow, ice and celestial blue, their sharp white peaks gently brushed every now and then by the tip of a long, aluminium wing. A kind of hush, an involuntary silence seemed to spread from them into the plane. At the back, people became quiet, observing an unofficial minute's silence, as it were, for that dead world, that other kingdom of snow. Hard by, on a ledge, I could

distinctly see a small military cemetery with a large tri-
colour flying over it. I thought I recognized one of the
many sad cemeteries of Resistance dead that there are
everywhere in those hills.

And now the golden, the rich, the fertile valleys of
France fell away from us, that fruitful, sun-drenched earth
responding so warmly to the spring and to thousands of
years of love, care and civilized attention. A long series
of peaks, broken and jagged, too low for snow and too
high for human cultivation, tossed us about like a life-
boat on a stormy sea. We came out into the still air over
Cagnes. A speed-boat was laying across the bay a curve of
foam that looked, on that sea so blue and still, more like a
smoke-screen across a noonday sky. A long way behind
us a plume of snow sank gently into the afternoon haze.

A steward called us for tea. I had forgotten how well
and how much my countrymen eat. The plumber, leaning
back over his chair, asked me if everybody ate like that in
South Africa.

I said: "Yes, most white people do." And he said:
"Crikey!"

Over Corsica, afternoon was turning into evening. The
ravines, which were deep, narrow clefts in the flanks of
steep mountains, began to fill with purple shadow. The
shadows of the peaks themselves lengthened and sped forward eagerly towards the distant sea; one sharp, volcanic
cone threw its bar of darkness right across a wide plain
which was still gold and gold-green with sunlight. The
first golden line of Africa appeared in front of us just as the
sun began to sink rapidly towards the horizon. Were it
not for that hour and for that light, such a vast quantity of
sand would have looked desolate and dull.

The plumber was obviously dismayed and disappointed.
"Is that the actual coast of Africa?" he asked.

"Yes, technically," I said, trying to comfort him. "But
you will hardly think so when you come back."

Were it not for the difficulties of speech in these planes, I would have tried to explain that what we were looking at was in the first place Mediterranean; secondly Levantine; thirdly Oriental; and only then, by the blind grace of geography, African. The more one knows of Africa, the less one feels this northern end to be part of it, and the more one knows the Mediterranean the more one sees its continuity even on these bleached and sandy shores of Northern Africa. The labyrinthine cord of an ancient culture, from Crete, Cyprus and Troy, from Greece, Carthage and Rome, was not broken even by the Normans, the Turks, the Arabs or the Moors. And as if to illustrate the point, the view began to produce something of Provence, of Italy and the European end of the Mediterranean. Some red-tiled homesteads, with pink and yellow walls, appeared, and silver-green orchards, and cypresses, orange-groves and vineyards. A tower of yellow stone and a honey-coloured wall held the sunlight for a moment. A flash of coral-pink and barbaric red shot across the western sky; and then over Tunis it was quite dark.

We landed at Castel Benito in time for dinner. But that same morning, only eight hours before, we had been in Britain and in the spring.

## Chapter Four

AT Castel Benito a new crew took over. Jakobus Gerhardus came to say good-bye.

That night the man who looked like my general, the plumber and I dined together in a restaurant built inside an old Italian hangar. The hangar was still pierced and holed in scores of places by the machine-gun bullets and bomb-splinters of the North African campaign. North African Italians served us, smilingly, with a large Mediterranean meal: with minestrone, ravioli, a fritto misto, tomatoes, pimentos, sabaglione and platefuls of large yellow apricots.

Afterwards we paced up and down the tarmac, watching the ground-staff refuel the plane under enormous arc-lights. Two N.C.O.s of the British military administration came and stood outside the hangar and watched also apparently speechless and half-asleep. The plumber suddenly went over to speak to them. Cigarettes came out, a lighter spluttered and broke into flame, and soon the three exiled heads were close together.

The business man then talked to me about Britain with some bitterness and much concern. He was typical of the best of his kind—and the best is so very good—and his anxiety was typical of the deep and growing concern for the fate of Britain that one encounters everywhere to-day. Whenever what Britain stands for in people's minds is felt to be threatened, in all sorts of unsuspected places, even among people who have no historical, economic or blood ties with Britain, this concern comes alive. I find it most moving. I was to notice it over and over again on my journey, to take heart from it, and to hope that we would be worthy of it. My companion now said nothing unusual.

He simply shared the general fear that Britain might be finished, that bad leadership, extravagance, inefficiency and bad workmanship had dealt it a vital blow. Above all he feared, hating himself for the fear, that it had become less honest.

I told him I could not believe that. A people as old as the British could not change their character over-night. There was much confusion, there were tremendous mistakes being made in Britain, but in the right cause. This latest vision of a just society could not be dismissed by argument, but had finally to be worked out in practice. Its worth had to be proved in an honest process of practical trial and error. I myself was stimulated and excited by post-war Britain. It was to me a remarkable proof of the spiritual vitality of the nation, that it could launch this great social experiment at the end of a great war of which it had borne the heaviest burden. Knowing Britain and its history, I was sure it would not fail.

I found it very important that at this moment a nation should try to be fair, good and true, and not merely an industrial sausage-machine in the great, mass-production manner, however profitable that might be. Southern Africa had already made one uneasy with its atmosphere of medieval privilege, a world of heartless white barons and black serfs. For how long did he think that would last, I asked him?

I had seen riots in Durban; I had seen in the suburbs of Johannesburg at nightfall terror creeping into the hearts of the European inhabitants. I had seen them bolt, bar, lock and re-lock their houses after dark for fear of what the black people might do to them. Almost everyone I knew in Johannesburg kept a loaded pistol handy. No white woman felt safe alone in a suburban street at night. Fifteen years ago it was not so. The writing, as a young South African had said to me, was up in neon signs all over the continent for people to read, yet people continued to believe that it could last indefinitely. Wherever we looked in the world to-day the whole of life was plunged into this great conflict: social good and private evil on the one hand, and private good and public evil on the other. I was more impressed than I could say, therefore, by this instinct of the British people, which made them give priority, at no matter what material cost to themselves, to a solution of this conflict.

I spoke, I am afraid, with considerable emphasis, for obviously none of us who care about the British way of living can be free of anxiety at this moment. I am sure that my vehemence put him off. I knew intuitively that he would mistrust emphasis just as much as he would avoid it in his own thinking and behaviour; probably the only emphasis he would understand was in moustaches, which was why his own was of a general's and not a subaltern's pattern.

"Well, I don't know, I am sure," he said. "It is all very difficult and perhaps you are right—but what about trying to get another drink before we push off?"

Two hours after landing we took off again. The plane had a new supply of petrol and oil, a new crew; its inside had been cleaned, dusted and sprayed and now smelt strongly of insecticide.

It was by this time very dark. For a while the lights of the town made a pretty pattern on the ground behind us, but they quickly disappeared. Soon there was no concentration of light anywhere below. Here and there the flash of a fire, a suffused glow, came up at us, but the intervals between one glow and the next lengthened rapidly.

When one's eyes had grown accustomed to the night, they became suddenly aware of the fact that down there it was all desert. At first one was surprised, because one had forgotten how hard the Sahara pressed upon the town and the surrounding land. For a long time there was nothing but the desert and the dark. But suddenly a new sort of light appeared, not an electric light but a fire of flame and

living warmth. It was unmistakable, and one's imagination and experience immediately surrounded it with
camels, black tents and Bedouins. The sight cheered and
warmed me. After a while another and then yet another
appeared, and then finally it became completely and
absolutely dark, and even that faint awareness of the desert
beneath us was dimmed.

The new stewards came round, took the last orders,
brought out extra blankets, lowered chairs and tilted them
as far back as they would go, helping passengers to settle
for the night. The plumber drank some South African
beer out of a bottle with a lion on it, which delighted him.
The business man had a double whisky and soda. "One
for the road, if you can call it that," he called out to me,
with an engaging smile.

"Better than a stirrup-cup," I said. "I wonder what the
equivalent would be for a machine like this?"

"Something for the tank," the plumber said with a
wink.

"Why not?" I remarked. "I had an R.A.F. pigman with
me in a Japanese jail who used to talk of twelve-cylinder
sows."

It all seemed so normal and commonplace, there, at
twelve thousand feet in the night over the Sahara. I wondered if it was quite right, and hoped it was not too
provocative.

The main lights were switched off. The curtains were
drawn across the windows. Only a few of the tiny reading
lamps in the side of the plane still shone their square beams
of light, illuminating a magazine page here, the knuckles
of a hand there. The aircraft stopped climbing. One
could tell it was high by the sting of the air in one's nostrils
and its taste upon the palate. The engines found the pitch
they wanted and settled down to a steady, rhythmical
roar. At last even the reading lamps went out, and it was
dark except for one blue light over the pantry door.
There we were, each alone in his own segment of the night.

I have flown many times by night. But I have never quite got used to that first moment in the dark when one sits with folded hands, alone, speeding through the air at a pace one cannot feel or adequately imagine. The night looks on steadily, its feet on the earth far below, its head in the stars. It is a solemn moment; sensations you have not felt and thoughts you have not thought since childhood come back to you. You feel yourself then to be really on a journey in the fullest sense of the word; not just a shifting of the body from point to point but a journey that moves through all conceivable dimensions of space and time, and beyond. For a voyage to a destination, wherever it may be, is also a voyage inside oneself; even as a cyclone carries along with it the centre in which it must ultimately come to rest. At these moments I think not only of the places I have been to but also of the distances I have travelled within myself without friend or ship; and of the long way yet to go before I come home within myself and within the journey. And always when the curtains are lifted, the night is without, peering in steadily and constantly, with the light of the stars far beyond.

Round about this moment it became apparent that we were not only flying over the desert but also through desert air. The aircraft began to pitch and toss violently. The stewards came hurriedly to the aid of their passengers. The hostess dashed to the children. Safety-belts were quickly fastened with complete impartiality round both waking and sleeping bodies. Lights flashed on and off. The children were the first to succumb, the older people were next.

The aircraft creaked and groaned like a ship in a gale and, even more alarming to amateur ears, the engines sounded as if they were beginning to beat irregularly, to shut off and cut in again with unexpected power at each new pitch and toss. At times one felt as if one were in a lift dropping down a vast shaft or through an empty hole in the sky. At other moments the machine flew up like a cork on an Atlantic comber or like the head of a startled stallion. A very fine dust began to fill the air. It became extremely hot.

To me, peering through the window, it looked as if we were flying through the smoke of an immense fire. I thought of a night in a thunderstorm over the Arabian desert when I was thrown far out of my seat, and hoped it would not happen again. Every now and then the exhaust pipes under the wings shot out large bright blue flames and showers of sparks. For a brief second I would see the wing trembling like an acetylene-green jelly or having a spasm of its own in thick swirls of dust. Those passengers who were not sick were soon tired from the violent movement.

The worst thing about it was that the plane possessed no recognizable rhythm which one's body could respond to, as in even the worst storm at sea. It was unpredictable; and so it continued all night. Dawn came eight hours later, flying up to meet us, smoking, surly, fuming with dust, high up in the air, while the desert down below was still in the dark. By then, everyone not prostrate was exhausted and possibly, like myself, somewhat frightened.

Just before sunrise, nearing Khartoum, we started to lose height with a sort of hoppity-skippity-hop motion. We were over the Omdurman hills, which always move me, not only because of the welcome variation they bring in the monstrous monotony of the Sahara, but also because history is here so near that one has only to stretch out one's hand to touch it.

They were still in shadow, but one peak looked, in that whirling mist, like a yellow rag of sunlight. I tried to point out the sights to the plumber, who of us all seemed least affected by the storm. I told him it was near there that the Lancers, and Mr. Winston Churchill with them, charged the Dervishes.

"What!" he said. "Our Old Winnie?"

"Yes," I said. "Old Winnie!"

"Old Winnie charged the Fuzzy-Wuzzies?" He seemed not to know the story.

"Yes! Against the Fuzzy-Wuzzies!" I answered.

He looked out again, shook his head, smiled, and said: "Good Old Winnie!"

Within a minute we saw the native town of Omdurman. It too was still in the shadows, but in scores of little brown courtyards, by the bare, unadorned mud walls of houses that looked exactly like cardboard boxes turned upside down, on the edges of the treeless streets, on the swirling sands of the desert itself, by the side of crouched camels, one saw hundreds of figures in what looked like white cotton nightshirts. They were all either prostrate on small square mats or were lifting their hands, then bowing, then lifting their hands again, in prayer to the East.

It had an extraordinary effect on one, to fly suddenly out of the desert and the night into a whole world at prayer. It filled one with tremendous respect for those people down below. I felt humble before them.

Our machine must have looked to those simple, impoverished black people below like the quintessence of human achievement as it flashed broad wings over their unpretentious homes. Yet if we looked back at the night we had just endured, it was not difficult to realize how much greater than the knowing and the assurance expressed in the speed of our plane had been that great darkness of wonder and unknowing without. Were those simple people below by any chance saying for us the prayers that we should have been saying? Had it come to this, that we Christians needed the prayers of the heathen?

It was here, then, that Gordon had been killed. There was the place, on the steps of his tumbledown palace, where he came out calmly to his death. There his head was cut off, stuck on a spear and carried out to the screaming and yelling Dervishes.

That moment stays with us, for there faith met faith.

That alone is how they meet. It is a law of the universe, it is a law like the law of gravity. Faith yields only to faith; faith begets, succeeds and replaces faith. Faith creates, all else destroys. Nothing else works. Our bright and glittering knowing by day induces an equal and opposite unknowing by night. But faith is knowing both ways.

> *It is the not-yet in the now,*
> *The taste of fruit that does not yet exist*
> *Hanging the blossom on the bough.*

It is this faith that I have always loved about this part of Africa. To me Omdurman and Khartoum are not distant places, but towns on the marches of my own Africa, for whatever the nature of the trees, Africa is all of the same wood and of the same interlocking pattern. Further, these particular places are essentially created by faith.

Over the river, just past three small feluccas on whose narrow decks more figures in white nightdresses were at prayer, we passed the place where two young naval officers, Hood and Beatty, had lobbed shells from their gunboat into the massing Dervishes. Both of them are now dead. Hood, a gallant, sensitive gentleman, went down with his flagship in 1914 during that other Great War, one of the earliest victims of German submarines. He went to his death as calmly as Gordon had done, refusing to leave his ship or to be rescued when others had to die. Beatty, a different type of man, who wore his spirit as jauntily as he tilted his cap over his eye, lived out his faith on the bridge of his flagship that day when he said: "There seems to be something the matter with our ships to-day", and made this signal—the last of the action—

KEEP CLOSER TO THE ENEMY

Close to the river, too, was that immense railway-line stretching back across the desert to Wadi Halfa. It, too, was an act of faith; Kitchener's faith in two junior lieutenants of the British Army, and their faith in themselves and the general plan and the feel of it all.

When I told the plumber that the line had been built by two subalterns with scores of uneducated, black workmen, he understood at once what this meant, because his experience and interests in life could readily assess the achievement. He exclaimed: "It would take a ton of brass hats and an army of sappers to do it now!"

Then there was Khartoum itself. We came down low over the housetops and we saw the streets, spread out on the pattern of a huge Union Jack as Kitchener meant them to be. What was that if not a symbol of the faith which moved at the back of his cool, far-calculating mind? As a result, there to-day on the west bank of the Nile is Omdurman, the product of Dervish, of Oriental-Africanized faith, and Khartoum on the east, the product of Christian, of Western faith, staring at each other, with what seems like mutual respect in their regard.

We landed between the golf-course and the town just as the sun came up. A native immigration officer and a native customs officer quickly passed us through the controls. One look at the sky made it plain that they were anxious to get us away as soon as possible. The dust was already whistling across the aerodrome and pattering like hail against the windows.

We drove quickly through deserted streets to the Grand Hotel on the banks of the Nile, where we were promptly served with a powerful breakfast. My companions, their senses still reacting to the violent experience of the night, ate what was put in front of them with a dazed, bewildered air, as if they really did not know what they were doing. A meal consisting of paw-paws, large plates of porridge, fried Nile perch, bacon and five eggs each, roast potatoes and tomatoes, toast, marmalade and steaming coffee, was set before them and consumed with impressive dispatch. I could not face such a meal in that heat and at that hour, so I went and walked around for a while.

I stopped to look at places I had known in the war. It was obvious that all memory of us had faded. Floating on the river in front of the hotel was still the same house-boat which used to take the overflow of senior officers from the main building. Now its empty windows stared blankly at some obscene Maribou storks standing in the dust on the far bank of the river, with their heads tucked into ruffled feathers. I walked to the house near the hotel where I had spent many happy days far from the war with books and comfort; but my friends had gone. There was a new name on the plate by the gate. The garden, however, still looked as English as a garden could possibly look there in that sun. This garden, it seemed to me, and the look on the faces of the natives had not changed in the least. Despite what I had heard and read, it was still the same frank, friendly, inquiring, manly look that I had always enjoyed so much after that strange, squint-eyed Egyptian glance. That look gives the lie to the people who say that there is something wrong in the relationship between the native and the European in the Sudan. It was always better there than anywhere in Africa; there is an essential rightness about it which is absent elsewhere.

I thought of my Sudanese camel-men in the war. I had been given very definite orders that when I got through into Abyssinia and reached the great Gojjam escarpment, I was at once to send back to the Sudan my camels and camel-men, who were civilians from Kordofan. I was told that at the foot of the mountains I would find mules and Abyssinian muleteers to take over my loads and go on with me. However, things turned out otherwise. When we reached the foot of the mountains we found neither mules nor muleteers. Furthermore, our arms and supplies were desperately needed. We decided to disobey orders and to take the camels on into the mountains. As the camel-men were all civilians and I could not order them to go on, I asked for volunteers.

By that time they had all done as much, if not more,

than they had ever contracted to do. A number of them
were ill with malaria, dysentery and tropical ulcers;
others had sores and festering feet. And worst of all, up
there in the foothills they were miserable with cold at
night. Some had pneumonia, some had bronchitis and
all had colds and coughs. None of them had anything
to wear but thin cotton smocks torn and tattered on the
journey.

They were in such a state, in fact, that some of my
European officers protested against my decision to take
them on. An officer with me, who was killed a week later
by an Italian bullet, felt so strongly about it that he refused
to interpret for me. Nevertheless I had called all the
Sheiks to my tent, where we talked it over frankly and at
great length. After many hours the oldest of them suddenly spoke up firmly: "Effendi," he said, "we have come
a long way with you. We are far from our homes and we
have done all that we promised to do. We are sick; we are
cold; our feet are tired and full of sores. But I am older
than any of these people here. I can remember what it
used to be like before the Government came. If the Government wants us to go on, we will go on." This phrase
"Before the Government came" stuck in my mind. I
found the phrase most significant. Subsequently I came
across it over and over again.

Now I looked at the people of Khartoum and exchanged a few polite words here and there; I saw them go
about their humble occasions without fuss or compulsion;
saw them lie down on the ground so confidingly and instantly go to sleep underneath those immense trees that
had been planted by their shade-obsessed rulers as a
matter of course in that desert where no trees grew before.
And seeing all this I could not believe that the phrase had
lost any of its validity.

How I envied them their sleep just then. It is the best
thing to do during the Sudanese day, which is no friend to
man, dog or tree. Already the day was piling up over the

town into a monstrous assertion of heat, dust, glare and aggressive power.

We were hurried back to the aerodrome. A few officials with their wives were there now to see the plane off. It looked as though it were a daily ritual for them, the moment when their homesickness had a brief, vicarious cure. They looked worn and rather listless. They watched us go with a wistful, condemned look on their faces.

In a few minutes, rocking violently, the plane was back in the sky, in the dusty, turbulent air over the town. But the morning before, at that hour, we had been in England and in the spring. That knowledge must have been there on our faces to be read enviously by those pallid exiles below.

# Chapter Five

I HAD looked forward eagerly to the part of the journey we had now begun. We had to fly south-east from Khartoum over country I knew comparatively well and which I had not seen for several years. In particular I had hoped to see for the first time from the air some of the country which I had so slowly, painfully and rather precariously crossed with my camels on the way into Abyssinia nine years before. But I was to be disappointed.

Once in the air over Khartoum the pilot of our plane wisely put it at once into a steep climb. Even an amateur like myself could see that it was not the sort of day for hovering close to the ground, and that the sooner we got into steadier air the better. For a while I was able, despite the wind and the dust below, to distinguish a few land-marks in that featureless country, but very soon, as we steadily gained height, the land lost all character and coherence.

Little more than a mild, yellow, unrelieved glare stared back at me from the earth. Soon we had again the sharp sting of air in our nostrils that we had had the night before.

One of the elder women in the plane suddenly went very white, started to moan to herself, and had to be given oxygen. The plane flattened out and the engines got back to their more comforting deep-throated roar. We had stopped climbing, but even at that height the air, although not so agitated as it had been the night before, was far from steady. The machine kept lurching, staggering and dropping unpredictably. I do not think that anyone felt really comfortable, and many of the passengers were sick. The element of the unpredictable in the external circumstances of our flight now seemed to enter into the minds of the passengers. They began to do things which they would not normally have done.

The men suddenly started drinking. Although it was only seven-thirty and although we had all just eaten far more than was good for us, bells were suddenly rung for the stewards, and beers, whiskies, gins, brandies and sherries were ordered, as if we were about to be served with lunch. One of the commercial travellers, while drinking a double brandy, began pulling letters and documents out of a case and tearing them to bits. I heard him say afterwards that he did not know what possessed him, for he had destroyed several important papers.

The Army nurse said later: "I don't know what happened. I seemed to have a black-out and then came round to find myself sitting on the lap of a strange man, drinking a large whisky." The plumber, I am sure, did not usually have so much beer at that hour, nor did he normally chain-smoke in that manner. On solid earth the business man would not have swallowed so much whisky. And certainly he would not have stared so at strangers, particularly not through horn-rimmed spectacles placed, in such a precarious and unmilitary fashion, on the tip of his nose.

For a while something unexplained and irrational appeared to dominate the actions of all of us. My own reaction was to concentrate more than ever on what I could see of the world outside. With my maps handy on my knees, I continued to look down with fierce concentration, as if I expected the haze and dust to vanish at any moment and a promised land to appear. After an hour or two I had my reward.

I noticed that the dust had gone and that a world of level, white cloud had appeared beneath us. Far to the east a peak or two of the formidable Abyssinian escarpments pierced through the cloud. I could not identify them from my map. The maps of Africa betray how young and incomplete is our knowledge of the continent.

Beyond the peaks on the horizon to which we were heading, and above this white, level world of cloud below us,
I saw a tremendous array of curling, twisting and turning
cumulus cloud. It stretched as far as the eye could see,
like a battle formation at the twilight hour of the Nordic
gods.

It was a most beautiful and impressive sight, but at that
hour it made me fear for this lap of our journey. In our
kind of plane, with the load we carried, I could not see
how we could possibly fly over those far-flung, those dense
electric Himalayas of cloud, and through them we could
hardly attempt to go with any degree of safety.

They were very like the great monsoon clouds that
sweep down from Burma and Northern Malaya over the
Bay of Bengal. Once, on an occasion like this, a pilot of a
flying-boat I was in refused to fly into them because he had
known a flight of five R.A.F. planes attempt it once, and
only one had emerged intact on the other side.

Shortly afterwards I realized that the pilot of this aircraft must have reached a similar conclusion, for suddenly
we changed course. Instead of flying south-east, as we
had been doing, the plane was now going due south, and
for several hours we flew parallel to that great range of
cloud. Nevertheless, without a split, a break, a pass or a
valley appearing anywhere in its formation, it pushed
steadily towards us. The atmosphere grew slowly darker,
chillier and more ominous because of its grim encroaching
presence.

Morning tea-time, that abiding, almost fanatical ritual
of Southern Africa, was observed elaborately on the plane
with trays full of fruit cakes, chocolate cakes, cream-
sponge and walnut cakes, pastries rich with cream, with
jam, custards, marzipans and icing, with half a dozen
varieties of sandwiches, with fresh fruits and, of course,
with cups of Nile-red tea. Just after all this had been consumed, at about noon, the clouds below us were suddenly
parted and Victoria-Nyanza appeared.

Kampala and the airport were almost exactly underneath us; a long way down, but unmistakable, the blue
waters of the greatest of the African lakes, unrippled and
serene, stretched away south of us as far as we could see,
unimpeded by land of any kind. With the view I felt a
rush of affection for Africa. Africa is great and majestic
in all it does, there is nothing mingy or mean in its methods,
no matter whether it is producing desert, mountain, lake
or plain. One could, at the same time, almost hear the
relief which filled the cockpit at that moment. The aircraft, losing no time, immediately did a determined and
quick bank to the east, and put its nose into a long decline.

The range of cumulus came up dead in front of us. The
pilot clearly intended to fly underneath it, now that he
knew precisely where he was. The green hills and the
green valleys, the well-watered, succulent vegetation of
this part of Africa lay there for our desert-worn and cloud-
dazed senses to enjoy. But not for long. Wherever one
looked, the horizon was black, purple-silver and pearl-
grey with cloud. The far hills were already grey with rain
and mist.

Up the valleys and down the plains, over mountain-tops
and across rivers, the storms came striding towards us.
Those lovely smaller lakes of the highlands of Kenya,
whose deep-blue waters are so heavily burdened with
sunlight and cloud and pink flamingos along their shores;
those snow-capped towers of Mount Kenya; those snug
homesteads and blood-red roads going from nowhere to
nowhere through bush and plain, were now all hidden
from view as completely as if it had been night. Bumping
and driving hard through heavy rain, we hardly saw land
again until some hours later we climbed with relief out of
the plane at Nairobi.

I said good-bye to my companions at the aerodrome.
From now on our ways divided. I had to spend the night
in Nairobi and then take a smaller plane on towards my
destination, early the following morning.

It is one of the more unjustifiable pretensions of our age that it measures time and experience by the clock. There are obviously a host of considerations and values which a clock cannot possibly measure. There is, above all, the fact that time spent on a journey, particularly on a journey which sets in motion the abiding symbolism of our natures, is different from the time devoured at such a terrifying speed in the daily routine of what is accepted, with such curious complacency, as our normal lives. This seems axiomatic to me; the truer the moment and the greater its content of reality the slower the swing of the universal pendulum.

Let me give an instance. I could imagine a moment denied to a life as soiled as my own—a moment so real that time would come to a standstill within it, would cease to exist despite all the ticking of clocks that went on. I do not want to claim too much for this humble, this unwinged moment there on the aerodrome at Nairobi. But I must emphasize, as best I can in dealing with a reaction that is beyond the normal use of words, that there was more to it than a mere twenty-four hours measured on the clock. Somehow the barriers between all of us had been down, the masks over our eyes had been lifted and we had become genuinely and unusually well-disposed to one another.

I now found myself borrowing pen and paper from a reluctant and harassed immigration officer in order to give to the plumber addresses of some of my oldest friends in Johannesburg. I also gave him a note of introduction to the managing director of a group of mines.

I exchanged addresses with the business man. We shook one another warmly by the hand and promised, without fail, to meet again. At the barrier his motor car was waiting. The business man pointed to his black chauffeur, who was grinning with delight, his eyes shining with excitement: "Send me a telegram, any time. Doesn't matter how far, I'll send him to meet you," he said.

# Chapter Six

As I left the aerodrome by myself to go to the town I experienced a sense of anticlimax. I felt as if the day had suddenly been emptied of the meaning it had possessed in the morning. The reaction was encouraged in me by Nairobi itself.

I have never known Nairobi well and yet I have been to it often, over a period of many years. I went there for the first time twenty-three years before, with William Plomer[1] and Katsué Mori, the captain of the ship in which the two of us were travelling to Japan. I was there again on my own for a longer stay some years later. I was there in the war on my way out of Abyssinia. Once I spent three weeks in hospital there with malignant malaria. I had been there only eighteen months before on my way back from the Far East; on that occasion I had arrived there so exhausted after a wild and long flight by York that I had fallen asleep in a chair by the fire in a hotel lounge. But no matter how the circumstances of my visits or my own state of mind varied, I have always had the same flat, uninspired reaction to it.

As a town it is pleasant enough and comfortable enough, but frankly unworthy of the country around it. One must go outside it and climb the blue hills in the distance, or

---

[1] Apart from feelings arising out of a life-long friendship with William Plomer I believe no one with any sense of the quintessential Africa can be unconscious of a very great debt to him. His was the first imagination to allow the black man of Africa to enter it in his own human right. Even the great and good Olive Schreiner saw the native primarily as a social and ethical problem. Plomer was the first to accept him without qualification or reservation as a human being. His stories of Africa are tremendously brave pioneer achievements and broke the first shackles in the European mind-forged manacles of Africa. Books like *Cry the Beloved Country*, or my own *In a Province*, would not have been possible but for him.

travel along one of those dusty roads leading out of it in order to get the feel of the vast and immensely exciting physical presence of the Africa by which it is surrounded.

Like so many towns of this century, Nairobi has discovered the deadly, the all too facile secret of growing without changing. Such places are the architectural equivalents of those earliest and simplest cells of organic matter which reproduce themselves indefinitely by the mere process of growing bigger and then dividing into two exactly similar halves. They are towns whose mounting sky-lines seem untroubled by doubt or imagination of any kind. Nairobi was no exception. It seemed to me unchanged, and left me rather indifferent.

And yet Kenya itself and its people are not of a substance to which one can be indifferent. They have between them the knack of rousing passions and excitements far beyond their own frontier, in a way unequalled in any other part of the continent. The people of Kenya appear to live in a permanent state of agitation, of frenzy, rage, rebellion and resentment, against various facts and circumstances of their daily lives. Much of this is understandable, because their circumstances are not at all easy, nor is their existence always pleasant. But over and above this consideration, there is something about the texture of life in Kenya which appears unrelated to fact.

It may be that the Europeans of Kenya are trying to live a fantasy. Perhaps they pursue, in the un-English setting of Africa, a dream of English country life which has long ceased to exist even in Britain. One feels that an important part of their lives is dominated by nostalgia. They are obsessed with a memory which is of no further use to them.

The many people in Kenya whom I know, like and admire, all have a queer, slight, but definitely somnambulistic air about them. They are not the lazy, pleasure-loving, decadent creatures that so many people in Britain think they are. In fact, Kenya is full of brave, hard-

c

working Europeans who, despite many disappointments, retain their sense of individual adventure. But they tend to behave at times like people walking in their sleep, and many of their excitements are dream excitements.

They themselves are the first to admit that they are a bit eccentric. They take quite a conscious pride in their eccentricity, and put it down, among other things, to the altitude. It is true that the Europeans on those far, blue-and-gold uplands come as close to being an air-borne, a sky-dominated community as is possible anywhere on firm ground in Africa, except in Abyssinia. And the Abyssinians, as I have good reason to know, lead lives dominated by fantasy. So perhaps there is something in what the people in Kenya say about the effect of altitude on European character. But there is a third factor that should be considered, which is everywhere overlooked in Africa.

We hear a great deal about the devastating effect that the European has on the native in Africa, but no one has ever stopped to inquire into the effect of the native on the European. The interplay of forces set in motion by that vast concourse of black, primitive people living so intimately with a small handful of white people. Those admirable women anthropologists, who examine year after year with such indefatigable ardour the tribal patterns, the sexual habits, the cats'-cradles of primitive Africans and the impact of European culture on them, could with profit and perhaps greater accuracy measure the effect this impact has had on their own patterns of behaviour. For it is by no means a one-sided business. Some of us who have been born and bred in Africa are well aware of it.

People like myself, whose first memory is of a large, black, smiling, crooning, warm, full-bosomed figure bending over his cot and whose friends for years were naked black urchins, know that contact between Europeans and Africans is, whether the individual wishes it or not, a significant, almost measureless two-way flow of traffic. The traffic can, with proper understanding and tolerance, enrich as well the life of the European. Or he can, with his own blind intolerance, divert and disorganize it to his own impoverishment and embitterment, as my countrymen do in Southern Africa.

I could easily make this the subject of an entire book. Similarly I am tempted to ask, why do so many women of great intellectual attainments nowadays have this interest in anthropology, in primitive behaviour and in unearthing the buried cities of Africa from the dust where, as D. H. Lawrence once said so meaningly, we have buried with "the silent races and their abominations, so much of the delicate magic of life"?

But it would be going too far beyond my immediate purpose.

All I must do in justice to this image of Africa, that for good or ill walks like a sunset shadow by my side, is to draw attention to the fact that the fantasies of those few thousands of white people among millions of blacks are influenced to no mean extent by their contact with the primitive. One sees it in the records of European crime in the colony. There have been murders committed by Europeans in Kenya that have a singularly uninhibited, primitive, almost innocent quality about them. There have been feasts and celebrations there inspired not only by Claridges or the Ritz but also by the kraals of African royalty.

Quite apart from the abnormal ones, the so-called normal aspects of European life in the colony suggest that conventional morality has lost some of its power, that people's appetites are given an importance and a licence they do not have at home. There is a love of eating and drinking, feasting and hunting, a love of collective excitement, of tribal agitation, of the unorthodox in dress, of leopard-skin waistcoats, cheetah tobacco pouches, of zebra and snake-skin hatbands, of crocodile shoes and hippopotamus-hide whips, of elephant-hair bangles, of

animal-skin rugs on the floor and the heads of lion, antelope and buffalo on the walls, of excess of all kinds, that is
in part the result of the contact with black people around.
It seems as if the presence of the primitive and of people
living far down in themselves and in time helps and encourages the Europeans to climb down from superior
altitudes in themselves.

Nor is it an accident, I believe, that, like his black neighbour, the European leaves a very heavy, a disproportionate
burden of the daily practical work to his women. These
settlers' wives in Kenya are amazing. I raise to them a
light, humble, European hat, officer's demobilization
pattern, without snake or zebra skin round it, with great
sympathy, respect and deference.

The point is that in Kenya one cannot for long escape
this paradox. The country is full of people whose emotions
and fantasies are most deeply engaged in their manner of
living, and yet whose towns, like Nairobi, are completely
without fantasy, emotion, character or colour of any kind.

After waiting for nearly three hours on the doorstep of
the Norfolk Hotel, at last I got into the room there which
had been booked for me by cable three weeks before. I
had to wait because there were two desperate men in it
who refused to leave because neither in that hotel, nor
anywhere else in town, was to be had a room of any kind.

The two men would not move from the room and
naturally I refused to budge. In the end policemen were
called to dislodge them. At that stage I withdrew discreetly, as I had no wish to see my two gallant opponents
fall back on such unprepared positions. The police, I believe, gave them a cell for the night, not out of revenge
but out of compassion.

Meanwhile I wrote my name in the Hotel Register,
which resembled nothing more than a selection of pages
from Debrett or the Navy, the Army and the Air Force
lists. I then moved into my room, where I was joined by
two other men who had booked it six weeks in advance.

The three of us agreed, after more argument, to share it for the night.

This setback robbed me of all desire to rest. I set out at once to track down Peter Brinsley-White, an ex-cavalry officer who had been one of my guerrilla group in the war in the East.

He had an office in one of those midget skyscrapers which all towns in Africa, despite the surrounding open spaces about them, put up as an indispensable badge of their devotion to progress.

I found Peter a little older, less harassed, but except for his dress otherwise essentially unchanged since I had last seen him. Even in the jungle he had always been most fastidious and meticulous, almost too conventional about his appearance. But now he sat there by me, behind a most imposing desk with the latest American office devices, dictaphones, adding machines, inter-office telephones of white ivory all round him, dressed in bright green corduroy slacks, red silk socks, black suede ankle boots, and a red, yellow and black checked lumber-jack shirt rolled up at the sleeves and open at the collar. His hat hanging on the peg by the door had a vivid puff-adder's skin around it. His moustache was twice as long as when I had last seen it.

We talked long and enjoyably over many cups of sweet, thick red tea, and then Peter said suddenly: "I wish, old chap, I'd known you were coming, but I've got to go to this blasted meeting to-night. It's most important. It's absolutely vital; it's about those finger-prints, you know!"

At the word finger-prints I could not help noticing as he said it a well-known look of battle come into Peter's eyes.

"You know about them, of course," he added.

I shook my head.

"But surely you do! You must be joking. I would have thought the papers in London were full of it. Surely *The Times* has told you all about it?"

I said I thought not, and as he looked so dismayed and unbelieving I asked him to tell me about it.

The entire country, he said, was in a passion about it. Some two years ago the Legislative Council had passed a National Registration Bill with everyone's consent. Some two months ago, when it was about to be put into effect, they had discovered it meant that Europeans, as well as natives, would have to have their finger-prints taken for the purposes of the registration.

"And, of course," Peter said, "we just won't stand for it. We're organizing. We've got chaps coming from all over the place. They're pouring into town. We'll make those bloody officials retract. It's just like them, slipping such a fast one on us. But we'll go to London, to Downing Street, to the Privy Council, petition the King, if necessary. But are you sure you didn't read about it at home?"

Poor Peter! I had never before, even in the worst sort of crisis, seen him like this; but I recognized the symptoms, and thought: "Whenever I am in Kenya there is something like this."

The first time William and I came to Kenya the country was in a passion about Norman Leys' book *Kenya*. We had great difficulty in getting a copy. We got it in the end from a man who, after first professing to be without it, brought it to us carefully wrapped in a mackintosh. He begged us not to tell anyone that he had lent it to us. Later it had been a "pyrethrum" scandal; and then it was the Indian vote. During the war it was a murder trial, for which such an assembly of distinguished witnesses was needed that even the Headquarters of the Army in the middle of Abyssinia had to surrender a quota of its staff-officers. Afterwards, the fourth or fifth time, it was amalgamation with the adjacent territories, and a host of other things. To-day it was finger-prints.

As I left Peter's office, I tried to retrace as nearly as I could the course of a curious search that William, Katsué Mori and I had conducted in the town twenty-three years before. Mori was convinced that somewhere in Nairobi he could buy bracelets made of lion's whiskers, and he was determined not to go back to Japan without one. So on a hot, thundery afternoon in August, with a violent brilliant light pounding on the roof-tops and ricochetting off flashing white walls and blood-red streets, the three of us had gone out from the New Stanley Hotel to search for a bracelet of lion's whiskers.

Our quest was not an easy one. We spent hours in shops, while Mori, with the patient determination of his race and in the strangest of English, cross-examined reluctant Europeans, Hindus, Sikhs, Parsees, Goanese, Singhalese, Kikuyu and Kavirondo on the subject of bracelets made out of lion's whiskers. Towards sunset an Indian in a small shop in one of the bazaars sold him a bracelet made of black hair which he swore was lion's whiskers. To us there was nothing royal about them, nothing to show that they had ever shadowed the quick electric lip of a king of beasts, but old Mori was supremely happy. Proudly and triumphantly he held them up against the fading daylight. I wish I knew what they had meant to him, for one could almost see in the light of his slanted, child-of-a-sun-goddess eyes their supposed progenitor walking majestic and superb. It was as if the success was not Mori's but Japan's, as if the lion produced whiskers and paraded in the light of his eyes not for a man but at the behest of an emperor.

I walked down a street and noticed it was named after a man who had given us tea on the morning of Mori's great search. A little farther down the street there stood an impressive memorial to him. William and I had taken joy in a pamphlet of his on Kenya, particularly in the sentence: "The giraffe galloping on either side of my car, reminded me so vividly of prehistoric times." In those days he used to sell Nestlé's milk; now he was part of the history of the town, and no doubt in time would become prehistoric too.

And Mori, what was he now? Did he know what I had done to his countrymen in the war, what they had done to me, and what we had all done to one another? I think the war walked the shimmering streets with us that day twenty-three years before far down at an inexpressible level of our minds. The pattern is continuous; and night and day, for all our aboriginal unawareness, invisible hands work at it without cease. Mori liked both William and me as much as a Japanese could like Europeans. No difference of idiom or lack of regard, but a sense of hurt, injured human dignity set us apart.

It was impossible to walk with him through one of the towns of our people without becoming aware that at every step something was hurting him, trying to make him feel, by contrast, inferior, getting at him through his colour and his race. He must have noticed, as we did, the looks the Europeans gave us, saying so clearly: "I wonder what that Jap is doing here with those fellows?" He must have noticed in the New Stanley Hotel that people registered inarticulate surprise at his being there in their midst. Instinctively they sat as far away from him as possible.

Then too there was the Governor of the Colony. A few months before Mori had carried the Governor with his following of A.D.C.s and secretaries in his ship from Mombasa to Dar-es-Salaam, and had refused to take payment for their passages. This very morning he had been to Government House for the fourth time to call on the Governor, and again the Governor had been too busy to see him. It was no use explaining to Mori, as one might have explained to someone of one's own kind. He was convinced that he was deliberately being hurt because he was a coloured person. And in a sense he was right.

For days afterwards, I used to see Mori brooding, staring into the fierce Kenya distances as if he saw his answer coming from the far corners of the earth.

I am sure I need not elaborate, but I remember agreeing with William that "Chaps like Mori will counter this colour prejudice by a white prejudice; they will put a white hatred in its place."

Here in front of me now were the same streets, full of shops crowded with every conceivable produce of the African jungle. I thought how old Mori would have loved to raid and plunder them. The only difference was that there were more people; more Europeans; more Indians; more half-castes; more blacks; more, bigger and fatter motor cars. The proportions appear fixed and constant for the hunter as for the hunted. The Mori process goes on ceaselessly. Night and day the same injuries and bitternesses send eager, frantic hands to pick up the threads of the same sombre design.

While I was walking, the sun went down. The storms we had flown through in the morning provided a tremendous setting for this departure. I know of no part of the world which stages this daily drama better than this antique, this ancient, sun-drenched, sun-wise land of Africa.

## Chapter Seven

At four-thirty the next morning I heard a soft, but urgently persistent, African voice at my bedside: "Bwana! Bwana! Tea! Bwana! Tea!"

I had slept badly and spent most of the night, neither awake nor asleep, in that state which collects troubles from both the conscious and unconscious worlds. In the room next door, some men had played poker-dice all night. The dice still rattled as I shaved. My room-companions had come in late, full of whisky, still marvelling at its abundance and cheapness. I realized as I pushed my white mosquito net aside that I was beginning to feel rather desperate with fatigue.

For all the speed of our flying in what is universally regarded as God's free air, I felt imprisoned in my journey. I felt as if I was moving in a fixed, pre-determined groove down a dark, opaque shaft of time.

I came out of my room and on to the hotel doorstep, just as a red dawn came flashing up behind a ridge lined with very tall, very straight blue-gum trees. Their bark, as lovely and smooth as any young Nordic girl's cheek, went pink with the dawn. The spreading light clung like dew to their leaves. The street was empty. On a vacant, untidy lot some tattered black figures lay asleep on the dark damp earth.

Standing beside bags made of good old English leather at the door of the hotel lounge, and giving me suddenly the most genuine, cherubic smile of welcome, stood a man, a stranger to me. He was one of the biggest and fattest people I have ever seen, but there was nothing in the least repulsive about his dimensions. He obviously had a genius for being fat and a talent for being cheerful. He

74

wore his size naturally, it fitted his temperament like a glove. It reassured me in an odd way to see him there; to see someone in this town who obviously slept well at night. He was wearing a pair of neatly pressed dark grey flannels, Eighth Army ankle-boots, and a dark blue blazer with Guards' buttons. He carried a topee in one hand and a fly-whisk in the other.

"I take it," he said, "that you too are flying in this cargo-boat?"

I said that he was correct if he meant the Bristol freighter going south.

"Precisely," he answered; and then with a chuckle: "I wonder if it has occurred to you that we are taking to the air in a cargo-boat on Friday the thirteenth?"

It had not. But, as he drew my attention to it, I told him that thirteen was my lucky number.

"I'm most interested," he said. "How could thirteen possibly be anybody's lucky number?"

I explained that I was a thirteenth child, born on the thirteenth of the twelfth month. If there had been a thirteenth month I would have been born in that. I elaborated on happy coincidences of thirteen in my life.

"You astound me!" he said with such obvious relief that we both laughed. "But being perfectly serious for a moment, thirteen is *my* unlucky number. It haunts me, it pursues me with bad luck. I stopped one in the war on a Friday the thirteenth. My girl sacked me on the thirteenth. Even my waist-line expands in multiples of thirteen. Whose thirteen do you think is stronger, yours or mine?"

I said mine obviously because I was the older.

"Thank God," he exclaimed. "Do you mind then if I stick close to you for luck?"

At the aerodrome we faced another of those great African traveller's breakfasts, while the day spilled like a tidal wave over the horizon. There seemed to be planes going and coming every minute.

"Piccadilly Circus," he said, waving a piece of buttered

toast around. "The movement through here nowadays is quite incredible. There won't be room for a bloke my size soon."

From a nearby table a man, who had been staring at us, suddenly came over and said to me in German: "Have you forgotten me?"

I recognized a displaced person to whom I had given some slight help with his answers to the questioning immigration officers at Capetown about nine months before. But he was so changed, so much fatter and so prosperous-looking that I certainly would not have known him on my own. He had just flown in, and was on his way back to Germany to fetch his father, mother, brother and his two sisters. He had done very well, he said, and was very happy. "I am in business in Johannesburg now," he added.

"What business?" I asked.

"Oh, business, very good business," he said.

When he left, I turned to my fat companion and said: "There goes a displaced person, no longer displaced," and told him the story.

"It's all very well, this displaced person business," he remarked with unexpected bitterness. "But please tell me who is not a displaced person nowadays? This is the age of displaced people. The world is full of people who do not belong anywhere in particular. I am displaced. You, I'm sure, are displaced. Africa is full of displaced negroes. They give it a long name here as if it were something peculiar to this continent; they call it detribalization. But plainly it is just displacement. Who could be more detribalized than us British out here in Africa?"

I looked at him with new respect, and asked him to tell me more. It was simple, he said; there was not much to tell. He had first come to Kenya during the war, liked it and had come back. He had been in East Africa five years now, and had to confess he would like to go back to England. But he couldn't. He had felt out of it on his last leave there. His friends did not seem to know what he was talking about. He, on his part, hated "the lack of style, of elegance, of manners, the joylessness of life at Home". He said "Home" with such unconscious emphasis, and added, "And I found myself missing the black faces so."

He asked me about the theatres and the buses in London; the cinemas; the pubs, particularly the pubs round Cadogan Place, where his people lived, about the weather and the spring. And he said: "I would love to be there now." Then he heaved himself out of his chair, stood up slowly with great effort, and surveyed the aerodrome with a look that went far beyond it.

Our "cargo-boat" came taxi-ing towards us. It looked an exceedingly sturdy aircraft, with a robust fixed undercarriage and broad, sturdy wings, but it did not please my companion.

"Bumps like hell!" he said. He looked about him and pointed to a dozen or so people walking out towards it, all with the same mass-produced mackintoshes over their arms. "See what I mean! No style! No composure anywhere. They can't even wait to be called to the aircraft properly, but have to rush out there like a lot of sheep, just in case they miss something, or are done out of something. That is your displaced rabble for you. A suspicious, uneasy, unbelieving bunch!"

They may have looked a bit anonymous, but I thought they were nice, ordinary-looking sort of people. At that moment a loud-speaker summoned us.

We all climbed into the aircraft, strapped ourselves to our seats, and took off straight into the sun, leaving a trail of red dust over the aerodrome.

We circled the town, which was just coming to life. I remember in particular how very golden some bunches of bananas looked on the heads of a long file of native women carrying them to the market.

We rose over the hills just outside the town and swung south on our true course. There was no sign of yesterday's storms, no hint of cloud, wind or dust in the sky. We could see clearly and very far.

To the north the 17,000-foot mass of Mt. Kenya stood up distinctly with a long feather of snow in the centre of its blue mitre. Far to the south-east, Kilimanyaro was humped and crouched along its 19,000-foot summit, under a far greater burden of snow.

I thought what an artist Africa is in the way it displays its great mountains. The greatest of them are never jumbled together as they are in Switzerland, the Himalayas or the Caucasus. They are set in great open spaces, and around them are immense plains, rolling uplands and blue lakes like seas, so that they can see and be seen and take their proper place in the tremendous physical drama of Africa.

For it is a drama of great and absorbing interest, this continent of Africa, as we saw it that morning after the storm. It is a drama in the sense that the sea is one. I do not know of any country, except perhaps the far interior of Asia, which is, in terms of earth, of solid matter, so nearly the equivalent of the sea. There seems to be no end to it. One goes on for thousands of miles. One goes on until one's eyes and limbs ache with the sight and the bulk of it, dazzled by this inexhaustible repetition of desert, lake, escarpment, plateau, plain, snow-capped mountain plateau, plain, escarpment, lake and again desert. And one almost thinks and hopes that there will be no more of it. But in the morning, across the next blue horizon, there is more. And what is stranger still, it is there as the sea is there, in a right of its own that is indifferent if not unfriendly to man.

One cannot fly over Europe, as I had done only forty hours before, and fail to realize how close the earth and man are to each other, how much and how deeply in one another's confidence. This land below us did not as yet care much about human beings. It was as D. H. Lawrence —with that strange intimate sense of his for the character, the personality almost, of inorganic matter—called it, "a continent of dark negation". The native, whose brown huts, thorn-and-mud kraals tucked themselves discreetly with a kind of implied fear and trembling into the shelter of the hills and ridges there below, may be closer to it than the Europeans, but he too is not entirely at home. His spirit bows down before it, is over-burdened and exhausted by it. The only living things which look as if they really belonged to it are the wild animals. Between the animals and Africa there is an understanding that the human beings have not yet earned.

Over the Serengetti plain the pilot, out of goodness of heart, a desire to please his passengers and because it was such a beautiful morning, brought the aircraft down so low that we nearly touched the tops of the acacias.

"I wish he wouldn't do that," said the fat man, going quite pale: "I do get so sick."

As he spoke, the aircraft began to plunge and heave like a trawler off the Hebrides. We were indeed close to the earth. I realized suddenly that for a brief second I had looked almost straight into the antique eye of a large giraffe. It was staring at the plane over the top of an acacia tree with an expression composed equally of intense alarm and the immense curiosity of its species.

"That is why the bloody fool does it!" the fat man said with a groan, pointing to the giraffe and referring to the pilot.

Thousands of wild animals now came into view. Hartebeest, eland, zebra, impala, gnu, thousands of gazelle threw up their startled heads, and stopped grazing. If they were far away they just stared at the plane; but if close, first they bunched tightly together and then, as the aircraft came steadily nearer, they started desperately running in circles.

I found myself thinking of an incident in the war with the Japanese. At Leweeuliang in Java, when our light machine-guns on the left flank opened up on the Japanese infantry, they were completely taken by surprise. Instantly they had lost their heads and all conscious control. They had bunched just like those animals, and then started to run in circles, screaming with voices that sounded as if they came not from their throats but from their stomachs; and all the while we continued to shoot them down.

When in doubt, it seems, when in fear, when taken by surprise, when lost in bush or desert and without a guide, the human, the animal heart prescribes a circle. It turns on itself as the earth does and seeks refuge in the movement of the stars. That circle, that ballet danced down there by light, fantastic antelope feet was magic once. But what use is it now?

Farther on a furious rhino came charging out of a clump of trees. No circles for him to-day, no instinctive nonsense; the evidence of the noise of the plane is sufficient for him, or for any right-minded animal. There is no room for doubt. There is danger about and he will deal with it. We saw him disappear across the plain behind us, still charging the empty blue distances with undiminished rage, while his mate and her terrified young calf trotted energetically round and round a dark pool of water.

"That rhino," said the fat man, looking green, "reminds me of a bloke I knew in the Army."

A short while later we saw a lion with a very dark mane. He got to his feet and casually looked upwards, then seemed to shrug his shoulders and to flop down again with an air of intense boredom. As far as one could see there was nothing but this plain with a few acacias spinning like tops in their own shadows, and the animals.

But soon we had to climb out of it. The sun grew hotter and the bumping increased and so we were sent back into the cool, blue sky. The detailed earth fell away from us. It became more and more difficult to distinguish the herds of native cattle, the kraals and the narrow red ribbons of winding footpaths and earth roads.

We flew over lakes, that would be considered big anywhere except in Africa, over streams and long savannahs and over dry river-beds which were great gashes of red, yellow and white in the earth. It looked to me, as it always does, more eroded and scarred, drier and less friendly than it had looked the time before.

After about three hours' flying, we came down at Tabora in the centre of flat, featureless bush country infested with tsetse fly. We trooped into a dark, thatched room for the inevitable cup of thick, sweet tea, but the fat man did not come with us. He said good-bye to me on the aerodrome.

I watched him present his luggage to two enormous African servants wearing smart khaki house-coats. Their bodies seemed to purr with pleasure at his return. Then he climbed into a jeep with great slow dignity, pulled his topee firmly down on his head, and with the fly-whisk at his wrist, grasped the steering-wheel. And so he took himself and his love of style and elegance away into the bush.

We left Tabora within half an hour. I seem to remember listening at one moment to the keeper of the restaurant telling us that their telephone from the aerodrome to the little town was disconnected because a giraffe that morning had got his great, inquisitive head entangled in the wires. I remember thinking how ill and exhausted the man and his wife looked. The next moment I was back in the aircraft, flying again over the same sort of Africa.

As the heat increased and as the day advanced with a shattering, irresistible brilliance, we climbed ever higher into the sky. Over Lake Tanganyika we were so high that the great hills round it looked flat and featureless, and the waters of the lake itself shimmered, vibrated, trembled and danced more like a mirage in the desert than a liquid substance.

I tried to look south for the outline of the plateau that I had to explore, for it was not so very far away; but another great array of cloud, like that of the previous day, was marching up over the horizon. By the time we passed over

Lake Banguewelo the heat and the glare had rendered the view as featureless, for all its brilliance, as a mirror with nothing to reflect. Even at that height one was aware of the great impersonal forces pressing towards an inexorable conclusion; one saw the point of a natural argument based on a logic of desolation. Only Africa can put it so clearly. To add to that feeling, great veld fires, vast areas of burning bush and grass, now began on every side to erect immense pillars of smoke, piling up towards the sky.

In the aircraft, meanwhile, we continued our routine. We had some more tea, and then we had lunch. We drank a hot tomato soup, had a choice of cold hams, beef, mutton, sausages, brawn and polonies, and then of tomato, potato, avocado and lettuce salads, and finished with cold trifles, fruit, cream and Roquefort cheese. People smoked and drank and exchanged commonplaces.

Sometime after one o'clock we came down at Ndola in Northern Rhodesia. We had crossed a frontier without noticing it, for there is nothing like flying for showing up the artificiality of the barriers we set up against one another on earth. Africa itself takes even less notice than most continents of these lines drawn on the map. Africa hemmed in Ndola, pinned it down and kept it in its fitting European place as effectively as it had done to the other towns we had passed. Like them this town seemed from the air to have a look of pained surprise at finding itself where it was.

For me the place was notable mainly because the conversation that I heard at the aerodrome confirmed the impression I had had in the air. The rains had failed. It was desperately dry. The fear of drought was deep in people's eyes, in their blood and in their thoughts. A District Officer who joined us said that there would be a desperate famine among the black people before the year was out. Already food was short, and there was a long way to go to the next rains, let alone the next harvest. I heard the District Officer assure his audience that these famines

occur every three or four years. It seemed incredible that
we could have been offered such meals over the heads of
thousands who did not have enough to eat. This contrast
is so elementary, it has such a long and dubious history,
its injustice is so obvious, its dangers and the destructive
thinking it breeds are so well known, that one would hardly
have thought it possible for it to exist.

As we went on, the impression of desolation became
sharper. We were going deeper and deeper into the
southern winter. Here ground-frosts at night had joined
the work of drought and heat by day. The earth took on a
darker, a more unresponsive tinge. The smoke that came
up at us from the fires below seemed fiercer and thicker.
The afternoon wind, fitful and uncertain of itself, raised
more dust among the bushes and trees than its effort
deserved.

Lusaka, the capital, brought an unexpected area of
green to our notice, it is true, but the chill impression remained as the afternoon deepened and the sun sank
nearer to those koppies with which Southern Africa
equips each of its horizons. And sadness crept into one's
heart. It all looked so like the Africa, the plain, the
Vlakte, which my countrymen in the Union called in the
vivid speech of my childhood "Moedverloor se vlakte":
the plain where courage fails.

Over the Zambesi the purple valleys were filled with
mist; a veil of cold, frost-bitten air was being drawn over
the scene. As the air became increasingly wintry, the sun
found a hill and crept quietly and primly behind it, leaving
a warm glow of satisfaction in the sky. It was a view and a
moment with which I had so many associations that it was
not difficult for me to imagine what the reaction to it was
among the plants, the animals and the human beings
down there. How keen would be the sense of forgiveness,
of forgiving and being forgiven, which the hour of sunset
confers on all living matter, and not least on the harsh day
which has gone before.

We came down at Salisbury in the dark. I found myself taking part once more in a dreary battle for accommodation. Salisbury heaved and bulged with newcomers even more than Nairobi had done. It was friendly and well-disposed, but powerless in the face of this vast new human traffic which was assailing Africa. I had to share a room with three other men.

Next door once again a game of poker-dice went on for most of the night. At dawn a cup of tea was handed to me by a similar black servant, and it was all so like Nairobi, and had come about so quickly, that it took me some time to realize where I was. Before the sun had risen I was back at the aerodrome watching the mist lift slowly from the ground.

As I stood there, tired and feeling myself to be three-quarters fantasy and only a quarter real, I saw, as if it were a scene in a dream, a score of composed, very upright, neat, clean little girls, ranging in age from about seven to fifteen, in pigtails and identical school coats. They filed suddenly out of the door of the aerodrome building and walked tidily over to a large aircraft standing nearby. Quickly they disappeared inside, the door was closed and the engines of the aircraft roared into motion. As the machine came by me gathering speed, I saw a vague, perfunctory flutter of little white handkerchiefs from behind the cabin windows; the people round me answered them with an equally perfunctory flutter of larger handkerchiefs and the half-hearted waving of a few masculine hats. I heard someone near me say, "Yes, St. ——'s: good school, you know, better than we have here, and it's so easy nowadays to fly them to the Union."

The whole incident passed off without emotion, without tears or recognizable regret and even without a sense of the unusual, except the unusual degree of detachment with which it appeared to be viewed by the girls in the plane and their parents on the ground. But to me it was such an unexpected, such a surrealist addition to the traditional features of these wide African uplands that I found myself parodying a limerick:

> *"These are the young ladies called bright*
> *Who can all travel faster than light,*
> *They leave home to-day*
> *In a relative way,*
> *And come back the previous night."*

Soon afterwards my aircraft too was in the sky, heading east. All the morning there was mist between us and the earth, and it only parted just for a moment or two three hours later to let us glide down on the aerodrome at Chileka, in Nyasaland. I had my morning tea at Blantyre, seventy-two hours after leaving England.

I had travelled nearly 7,000 miles; I had passed from a spring of sunshine, of uncompromising and unending blossom, into an early and barren winter. I had not, it is true, travelled faster than light and I had travelled in an absolute rather than a relative way, but I felt as if I had come back much earlier than the previous night, at some unfinished, unresolved moment far back in the past; and I was more relieved than I can express to have done with flying for some months at least.

## PART III

# ENCOUNTER WITH THE MOUNTAIN

"O the mind, mind has mountains; cliffs of fall
Frightful, sheer, no-man-fathomed. . . ."

GERARD MANLEY HOPKINS

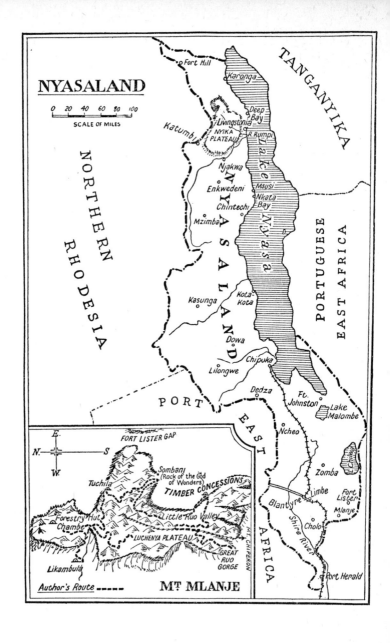

# NYASALAND

0 20 40 60 80 100
SCALE OF MILES

TANGANYIKA

Fort Hill

Karonga

Deep Bay

Katumbi

Livingstonia

NYIKA PLATEAU

R Rumpi

NORTHERN

Njakwa

Enkwedeni

Msusi

Nkata Bay

Chintechi

N
Y
A
S
A
L
A
N
D

Mzimba

L
a
k
e

N
y
a
s
a

RHODESIA

PORTUGUESE

EAST AFRICA

Kasunga

Kota-Kota

Dowa

Chipoka

Lilongwe

Dedza

Ft. Johnston

Lake Malombe

P O R T

Ncheo

E
A
S
T

Zomba

Fort Lister

A
F
R
I
C
A

Blantyre

Limbe

Mlanje

Shire River

Cholo

Fort Herald

FORT LISTER GAP

E.

N S

W.

Sombani
(Rock of the God of Wonders)

Tuchila

TIMBER CONCESSIONS

Forestry Hut
Chambe

Little Ruo Valley

M
T
.
C
H
I
P
E
R
O
N

LUCHENYA PLATEAU

GREAT RUO GORGE

Likambula

Author's Route ----

MT MLANJE

# Chapter Eight

IN Blantyre, the commercial capital of Nyasaland, I now found myself up against the same accommodation problem as in Salisbury and Nairobi. Blantyre and Limbe, its Siamese twin a few miles away, were in their small way as overcrowded and short of bedrooms as those other towns; and by experience less able to deal with the problem. Those other towns had a history of steady, energetic growth behind them; these places in Nyasaland had found their own leisurely, individual almost wilful way into the present, and were not used to this new scramble.

Before the last war, for people like myself, one of the great attractions of the Protectorate was its knack of being a quiet rule unto itself. It was one of the more neglected of the British territories in Africa. It attracted few of the attentions and none of the sensational publicity which some of its neighbours did. It roused little interest among tourists. The manly European heart, crossed in love, continued to show a marked preference for transferring its frustrated emotions on to the fauna of Kenya and Tanganyika. The League of Nations never grew particularly hot under its high international collar about Nyasaland. There, the problem of the European settler which so seriously troubled relations with the Colonial Office in Kenya and Northern Rhodesia appeared to be no problem at all.

Although there were close on two thousand Europeans in the country making a living out of planting tea, tobacco, coffee, trading and converting the African to Christianity, the difficulties they had with the odd thousand European officials who governed the country, and with their masters in Whitehall, were dealt with inside a tight and loyal family circle. The two-and-a-half million natives in Nyasa-land, on their part, seemed untempted by the growing African fashion of sending spokesmen or deputations abroad to appeal against exploitation by a white Imperialism.

The Protectorate, in fact, struck one as an unusually happy part of Africa, happy in the sense in which George Eliot defined a happy woman as being a "person without a past". I use "past" here not as a synonym of history. Nya-saland, of course, has a history. It has an exciting and highly individual history that bears comparison with most histories in the continent. If anyone is interested in that remarkable, inspired mixture of motives, the desire to trade, to serve God and the Queen and to rid the world of slavery, which brought the Victorians to Africa, he can see it displayed before him, like a rare insect under a micro-scope, in the history of the Protectorate.

The Protectorate was undoubtedly one of the better products of their mixed motives. Its own native history was a recurring pattern of destruction from which the coming of the British happily delivered it. But what the Protectorate does not possess is a past for international gossip to feed on. For half a century world curiosity ignored it. The great and growing traffic of Africa passed it by. Stretched along six hundred miles from North to South, little more in reality than an extinct volcanic strip round the great lake which gives it its name, and well off the main routes of the continent, Nyasaland grew quietly in its own individual way, with its own colourful variations of the sun, mountains, valleys, plain and remoteness of Africa; a far country only for the devoted, the more adult and athletic tastes to enjoy.

But times are changing now, and people are pouring into the country. The stories I heard about hotel-keepers' troubles at the reception desk in Ryalls hotel on this Satur-day morning of May 14, not only depressed me, but also filled me with alarm. I had to spend three months in the territory; winter was coming on. I decided that, as soon as possible, I would get myself a tent so that, if the worst came to the worst, I would at least have some shelter of my own. Meanwhile I gratefully accepted the loan of a back room, belonging to one of the permanent boarders who was away for the week-end, and prayed hard that something else would turn up by the Monday. My accommodation problem, however, was about to be solved in the happiest possible manner for me.

I had with me a letter of introduction to Alan Macbean, the director of one of the bigger departments of the government. While my room was being prepared I decided to go to his office and present my letter in person. Though we had never met, our trails had frequently crossed in the past in other parts of Africa and we had a number of friends and acquaintances in common.

Blantyre is a small, ugly, commercial town. It has not had much time, and no reserves of wealth, tradition or local pride out of which to shape itself. About sixty years ago the government dealt it an unkind blow by setting up the official capital on the side of the huge mountain of Zomba, forty miles away, and so robbed Blantyre of a sure source of dignity and self-respect. Ostentatiously, pointedly and rather disdainfully, it was left to get on with its business, and however well it may have done it, it looks to this day rather ashamed of itself.

Fortunately this tentative little town hides itself behind the ample skirts of its surroundings, so the memory left with me is of a series of vivid but inadequate fragments. After my strange, precipitate flight from England we had emerged out of a narrow pass between substantial dark hills, mist still in their laps, and driven straight into the centre of the town before I became really aware of it. I was surprised when the driver of the car said suddenly: "Well, this is it!" I do not know what I had expected, but obviously nothing quite as drab and insignificant as these hunched, perfunctory buildings dumped by the side of a road full of dust.

In the main street itself we had to go very slowly to avoid breaking the springs of our fat American car in the pot-holes. Behind us a thick, oily red dust rose up like smoke and spattered down like sleet on the trees, bushes, the glinting tin roofs and the sun-twisted wood of Goanese and Scottish shop verandas. The vegetation was grey and dejected with dust, the blanched faces of the whitewashed buildings smudged with it. The dust made many a black countenance a clown-like caricature of itself, and Indians and Goanese went turbaned and goggled against it. The sun made an unholy ally of it, and both sun and dust poured heavily, drunkenly over everything.

I admit, however, I had a more comfortable view of it now as I set out from the hotel for Alan Macbean's office. Away from that ugly, untidy centre, the town had more charm. The abrupt rises and falls in its wide background sheltered numbers of comfortable houses, all solidly built to an inoffensive office-of-works pattern. The houses gave on to gardens of a marked similarity. Each tried to have the same neat, level hedge round the inevitable lawn. I say "inevitable" because I believe, in Africa, the vision of an English lawn flies over the exiled British imagination like colours nailed to the mast of an out-gunned, sinking ship of the line. The lawns impinged on borders which grew European flowers of a sickly and outraged appearance. The only flower which seemed to do really well was the African zinnia. The lovely, effortless, uninhibited blooms, sizzling with colour and sun-fire like Catherine wheels at a fair, seemed to be sharing a joke of their own at the patient, determined nostalgia of the gardens about them.

The mist by now had gone from the dark hills round the town. Other and bigger hills, of a deeper blue, became visible and gave a suggestion of vast plains beyond them. The unflecked sky curved towards the dark earth with unimpeded rhythm, like a long, Pacific comber speeding towards some lagooned land. The town and its gardens, the confused blend of Goanese and British suburbia seemed to shrink to some vain and rather provocative gesture; to be no more than some very pink-and-white mouse rearing its head against the lowering, curved but as yet sheathed paws of an African cat. The image came to my mind unbidden and appeared confirmed by laughter which suddenly welled up like a spring around me.

I had not heard such spontaneous, pure and immediate laughter for years. I was turning down a road that had a halo of dust over it and was full of people doing their week-end shopping. Most of the few Europeans were in some kind of khaki, with set, sallow, lifeless, disillusioned faces under wide-brimmed hats. They climbed in and out of their cars with a listless, predetermined air. I had the impression that they all longed for nightfall so that darkness and drink would help them to imagine themselves to be some-where else. There were more Orientals than Europeans in the street and they, on the whole, were characteristic of a race which has a genius for appearing to be only half of what it really is. The Orientals all tended to have ascetic faces; finely made bones, delicate wrists and fingers; big, introspective eyes and a sensitive, gentle, defensive look. Their appearance, in fact, contrived to belie utterly the mercenary pursuits to which they dedicated their lives with such singular and indefatigable devotion. They had even less joy in them than the Europeans, and the laughter had come from neither of these, but from the Africans. These black people, overwhelmingly in the majority, carried the physical burden of the European and Indian day. They were, with few exceptions, dressed in rags and tatters which they wore not without pride and style. They talked with the greatest relish and animation. They were gay and laughed continually. Their laughter seemed to come straight from some sure, inviolate source within where one felt they were unfailingly refreshed and had the habit of feasting with kings. Their laughter matched the sun, the curve of the sky, and the sombrely burning land and—and this is why I have lingered with it so long—it flashed like some inspired revelation of the future over that incongruous street. The impression was still vividly with me when I walked into Alan Macbean's office.

I was shown into it without delay by a black clerk who was extremely courteous but, unlike his raggle-taggle countrymen in the streets, was bowed down by melancholy. This learned, self-conscious gloom which higher education inflicts, almost without exception, on an instinctively happy people, is most noticeable.

Macbean, a man of about forty-five, sturdily but not heavily built, with wide, steady but not entirely happy eyes, came to meet me. His appearance was fastidious and he wore his clothes as if they were some distinguished uniform. Pipe in hand, he looked more like someone about to take his dogs for a run over a Scottish moor than a tried and experienced officer of His Majesty's Colonial service.

"But where is your luggage?" he asked at once.

"At the hotel," I told him.

"But you must come and stay with me," he said firmly and warmly. "I suggest you just pop over and pay your respects to the Provincial Commissioner's Office. We are a little sensitive here and appreciate these courtesies. Then come back here and we'll collect your bags and go straight home."

The Provincial Commissioner's Office was recognizable at once for the neat, white flagstaff outside it, flying a clear Union Jack, and for the whitewashed stones by the main entrance, brilliant under the sun like the polished skulls in a Dyak village that I had once seen. The African messengers, too, in their starched uniforms, were unmistakable.

The Provincial Commissioner was away, but his deputy, young Charles Arbuthnot, received me on his behalf. He was not long out of the Army and was wearing white shorts and shirt. He sat at a desk of unstained African wood, a telephone at his side. The room was shaded against the light of the day which lapped, trembling like the clearest of water, at the rim of the window-sill.

Our greeting over, he startled me by saying suddenly: "You've come to do Mlanje and the Nyika, haven't you?"

My mission was confidential and I must have looked my surprise, for he said quickly: "I heard from the aerodrome you'd arrived. You see, this is my district. It's my job to know what goes on in it, and no stranger comes into it without my knowing. When I saw your name, I remembered that London had asked us to help. I remembered it particularly because I know Mlanje. I love it. I often go fishing there."

I was delighted with the chance of getting first-hand information and asked him many questions. He answered them well and at length.

He brought out a map and showed me Mlanje. "A big, a terrific place," he said. People vaguely called it a plateau, but from the little he had seen of it, it looked more like a collection of sharp, jagged mountain peaks from seven to ten thousand feet high. They were supposed to cover an area of from 120 to 190 square miles, but they had never been properly surveyed. It was, he said again, with a sort of schoolboy emphasis, "a terrific, a wizard, a grand place". He knew one small end of it, a peak and a bit of plateau called Chambe, where the "forestry people" had a hut and depot. "Lovely there; like a glen in Scotland; clear streams with rainbow trout in them." He went there to fish whenever he could leave "this awful town". But there was a good deal more to it than Chambe.

There was another part of the mountain, with a track leading up it from the headquarters—the "Boma", he called it—of his opposite number in that district; there were two or three huts here also. In fact, an eccentric old lady (eccentric only in the Nyasaland sense, he stressed with a smile, because she thought of doing things that had not occurred to the majority) had kept some cows up there.

But by far the greater part of Mlanje was not known at all. In the old days, in the bad season, quite a few hardy souls had gone up to places like Chambe to escape the heat of a summer which had to be experienced to be believed. Nowadays, with cars and planes, of course, they preferred air-conditioned cinemas in Salisbury and Bulawayo. "Only one or two queer people" like himself went there for fun.

No, it was not difficult to get at. It was only about forty-five miles away, just off the road to Portuguese East Africa. The difficulty was not to get there, but to get up it, and once up it, to get round it. That would be "quite an expedition" and need careful organizing and stout legs.

He wished, with a genuine look of regret, he could come too. But, alas, too much bumf! Look at it! Trays of it! Crying shame! He would, though, give me a letter to Martin Boyd, his opposite number at Mlanje. He was sure Boyd would help to get me carriers. They would be the great difficulty. The natives did not like the place. The mountain was too cold, too wet, too misty, and too high and steep, and it frightened them in an odd way. Did I realize that it was the native legends about Mlanje that gave Rider Haggard the idea for *The People of the Mist*?

"There was something tremendous about it," as I would soon see for myself. He grinned at me like a schoolboy, but suddenly becoming serious, said with a plenipotentiary air that he thought I ought to go and see Peter Quillan, the Provincial forestry officer, as well. He lived at Limbe, only a few miles away. "A charming person" but a "bit of a fanatic about trees". He lingered over this rather as if for emphasis. I had a feeling that I was being warned. The pause, the hesitation, if any, was well-nigh imperceptible, but I felt it was intended to convey something.

He then looked me straight in the eyes and added: "In fact, all the forestry blokes are dead keen on Mlanje. They feel rather special about it. There's another young lad called Vance, who looks after the forestry end of the mountain. He, too, is very keen, dead keen. The mountain means a lot to them, but I am sure you will get on with them all right."

I made a careful note of the "but" and said good-bye,

grateful for the luck which had brought me to so intelligent and sympathetic an informant.

I found Macbean waiting patiently for me. His solemn black official was already in the back of the car, looking a bit like African chaos and old night.

"A spot of trouble at home," he said, pointing to the official, "so I am taking him along. Jump in."

The hotel seemed delighted to lose me, and within three hours of my arrival I was in what became for me, on the rare occasions I was to be in civilized surroundings, my home in Nyasaland.

# Chapter Nine

AT the time of my arrival in Blantyre on this sunny, immaculate morning in May, Alan Macbean had been in Nyasaland about a year. Most of his career in the Colonial service had been spent in East Africa; twenty years or more of it in Kenya. I think he loved Kenya as much as a person with an inexorable sense of exile can love any country but his own. He did good and distinguished work there and left it with regret. He never told me, but I suspect that he left because of his children. He had two daughters. They were with their mother and at school in Scotland. Photographs illustrating their development from an East African cradle to a girls' college at home were discreetly but ubiquitously spread through the house: two charming, clean little Highland faces hung on every wall. Occasionally smiling, they were usually rather serious with something of that ancient, twilight, backward glance of the Gael. Their father had it too.

A few years before, the elder girl had recovered from a dangerous attack of infantile paralysis which had left her crippled. It had been a great blow to Alan. And it made him, a resolute person, determined that the best possible education that money could buy should make it up to her. When this offer of a government directorship in Nyasaland came along, he took it, not because he wanted to leave the Highlands of Kenya where he had been so long, but because it meant promotion and more money. He had thrown himself into his new work with great energy and efficiency. His department, which had been one of the most backward, had quickly become one of the best.

There has always been something very moving about this quality, uniquely their own, that so many of the best

Colonial servants bring to their work. One realizes clearly that many of them have had no chance to identify themselves permanently with any part of their Empire. Irrevocably, they have to uproot themselves from their own soil in Britain, and are never allowed to put down roots elsewhere. They have to make their work their home, although they must know that at forty-five or fifty-five, when they are forced to retire, the door of their own making will open and shut on them for the last time and leave them homeless. I am sure Alan was perfectly aware of what awaited him but, in the unavoidable, the cruel absence of a family life to which he was deeply attached, he too made his work his home.

The house in which he lived was for him little more than an outpost in his mind, a place in which to eat and sleep. With the discipline so characteristic of him, he observed all the civilized decencies. He made his house comfortable; furnished it with skill and not without taste; and made it for passers-by like myself a most welcome and endearing refuge. But I never felt that his heart or imagination was touched by it.

He left the running of it almost entirely to a remarkable Swahili servant, Ali, who had come from Kenya with him. His domestic staff consisted of Ali, a cook, a house-boy and a gardener, all black. No women were allowed in the house and Ali ran the staff with a hand of steel. He ran Alan, too, but rather as a nurse might run the eldest son of parents she respected and loved. Every day while I was there I heard Ali call Alan with his tea at five in the morning. "Jambo! Bwana. Your tea, Bwana. It is five o'clock." The deep voice spoke in Swahili, for Alan would not let him speak anything else.

At half-past five Ali would be back at Alan's door, knocking. Getting no answer, he would go in and say: "Auck Bwana! Your tea now is cold. It is getting late. Surely the bwana can now wake up!"

At six Ali would be back, knocking again, with fresh

tea. He would get no answer, walk straight in and say firmly: "You are doing wrong, bwana! This must now end. Here is fresh tea. It is six o'clock and what will your staff and clerks say if you are late? This is nonsense, bwana."

The "nonsense", the only English word he ever used in my hearing, always did it. With a great laugh and a heave Alan would be out of bed. At seven we had breakfast. At seven-thirty punctually Alan would be in the office. All through the day Ali ran the house with the greatest efficiency.

Frequently in the evenings Alan and Ali could be seen working in the garden together. It was a difficult garden, but between them they had grown the most wonderful beds of sweet-peas I have ever seen. The sweet-peas filled the hard, metallic air of Africa with a gentle, soft, nostalgic English scent. Every day I was there, Alan and Ali picked and arranged great, brimming bowls of them all over the house. Ali knew what those sweet-peas meant to Alan. He always called them the "English flowers" to me.

Whenever we left the house, Ali was there at the entrance to bow deeply and utter the Swahili farewell: "Kwa Heri, Bwana." Whenever we came back, no matter how late, at two or three in the morning, he was there waiting to let us in with great, good and dignified grace. He gave Alan something precious, something tender and human in his service that no other living thing did in Nyasaland, and I greatly respected him for it.

One of Ali's own, very special duties was to look after Argyle, a large, athletic young black cat Alan had adopted. Argyle was not only very handsome, but also understood human beings and their speech to a remarkable degree. Alan would sit playing with him for hours, talking to him with Argyle talking back, with growls, miaows, flashing paws, electric quivers and strange curvatures of the spine. Alan would not eat until Argyle had his bowl of food put before him in a corner of the dining-room. The only subject on which he and Ali appeared to have differences of opinion was Argyle. Ali thought he was too harsh with it.

Alan had a tiny whip of string made. When Argyle interrupted the conversation at table, Alan would lean over and flick him gently with the string. Ali thought this went much too far. In the evening at dinner, the whip was in its usual place but the string had been replaced with streamers of paper. Alan had tried repeatedly to revert to string but Ali would not let him. These three were the real world of that house, these three and the sweet-peas in the garden; all the rest stood on the fringes of Alan's mind.

On the Saturday of my arrival, after lunch, Ali immediately went off to fetch the black official who had come along with us in the car. Through the windows I watched a great discussion taking place between the servants under the blazing sun by the kitchen door, a grave, solemn and detailed discussion. Later, Ali and the black official knocked at the door and came quietly in.

"Well, what is it, Ali?" said Alan.

"I will leave it for him to say," Ali answered, pointing to the elderly official.

"I am afraid, Bwana," said the official in a lugubrious voice, "I have grave trouble to report . . ." and then paused as if he dared not go on.

"Come on!" said Alan. "Snap out of it. What is it?"

"I am afraid, sir! There is a grave dissension in your domestic midst. Your house-boy accuses his wife of promiscuous infidelity. By some extraordinary coincidence she accuses him of the same thing."

He outlined the history of the quarrel in the most excellent, pedantic English. The quarrel, he thought, was beyond healing. They had all talked it over and agreed there was only one thing to do. Here Alan looked at Ali and Ali nodded. They were sending the couple to their village to get divorced. They had arranged for replacements in the meanwhile and he could assure the bwana there would be no more trouble if that were done.

"But, I say," said Alan, breaking into Swahili and talking to Ali. "Isn't that a bit steep? Aren't you going too far?"

"No, Bwana," Ali said emphatically. "It is the right thing to do. It is not nonsense."

"Well, you see to it, then, Ali," Alan said, and dismissed the matter from his mind in a manner which was most flattering to his black arbitrators. But he said to me later: "That old clerk of mine is a marvel. I get him to investigate all my labour disputes for me. He settles them all according to the customs of the land and it saves no end of trouble. But he is not a patch on Ali!"

Afterwards, because Alan wanted to buy a carpet, we got into his car again and drove over to an auction sale of second-hand furniture in the tobacco market at Limbe. Alan said Ali was always nagging him about his carpets, and plaguing him to get more. Besides, these sales were fun. Everybody went to them. They were held every Saturday. As there was no work to do, one might as well go.

"There!" I thought. "When there is no work to do, the homelessness comes rushing in."

Alan drove the car, a powerful American make, with great, impatient speed but immense skill; he drove it rather as I suspected he drove himself: as if he did not care for the journey and the machine, but wanted it over quickly.

At Limbe we found the whole European world at the sale. It was held in an empty tobacco shed with something of the atmosphere of the Caledonian Market about it. And how incongruous it was to see there, in the heart of Africa, little heaps of soiled Victorian household things, outmoded Edwardian fineries, and in particular one large green-blue Japanese porcelain jar, with a vigorous and extremely elegant aspidistra in it. I confess I was astonished, and my imagination, when I thought of the immense tropical vegetation without, so stirred, that I stared at it as if it were the Livingstone, the Stanley of the botanical world.

In the end Alan bought no carpets. The prices and the colours were not right for him. His purse was too dedicated, his eye too fastidious. But we both of us met a number of old acquaintances, including a happy extrovert from Tanganyika who, with typical African disregard of time and distance, had thought nothing of motoring 1,300 miles to spend a week-end in Limbe.

The sale over, we drifted to the Club at Blantyre. European life in Nyasaland in its collective aspect turns on a well-organized system of clubs, and the Europeans we had seen at the sale reappeared at the club-house.

We all spread ourselves in the sun on the club veranda and watched a team of European officials and business people play a team of Indians and Goanese at hockey. The setting was rather beautiful. The hockey match was being played on what was normally the cricket field. It was at the bottom of a deep bowl in the Blantyre hills. We sat on the rim and looked down on it. The grass below was of the colour and texture of English grass. Had there been a spire in the background one's imagination could easily have turned it into an English scene. But beyond, and above the deep well of angry light, the hills were unmistakably African.

I do not know why it is that the many and varied peoples of India should all have such a genius for hockey. Nothing we know about the Indian character, its extreme, ancient and subtle complexities; its profound mistrust of simplicity; its capacity for making the obvious mysterious and complicated, prepares one for it; but the fact is they have a talent and passion for the game that make them far and away the best hockey-players in the world. The Europeans of Blantyre were soundly and decisively whacked. The spectators, essentially European, were scrupulously fair. They cheered the two sides impartially. When the Indians came off victorious, they greeted them with a genuine, a warm burst of clapping.

They looked a good, unpretentious, pleasant crowd, not

yet pulled out of proportion by Africa as were so many of their neighbours. But as I watched them I suddenly realized with a shock that they, and I, were all there, not because we really liked it, but in order to kill time. I have known the phrase all my life, but until that moment I honestly believe I had never fully appreciated its awful implications. I think it was meeting Alan, and the sense of the problem in him, that made me realize there were communities who deliberately set out to kill the time of which we all have so little. When the sun went down behind the hill and the damp, dark shadows welled up like a tide round the club-house, it was almost as if we had succeeded so well in our object that a faint, musty smell of death welled up with them.

There and then I decided that I would not waste a day on my journey; I would get up and down that mountain, and over my plateau as fast as I could; and so out of Africa.

When we were back at the house that night, sitting in front of a large log-fire, Argyle purring on Alan's shoulder, his eyes tightly shut with heat and ecstasy, a smell of meat grilling on wood-coals creeping in from the kitchen, I told Alan how important it was for me to get my work done as soon as possible. He, characteristically, without hesitating, took Argyle off his shoulder, gave him to me, and without saying a word went out of the room and started telephoning.

"I have been through to Zomba and they will see you to-morrow," he said when he came back. "It will fit in quite well because I am playing golf. I have also rung up Boyd at Mlanje. He was just going to telephone you. He had already heard from the D.C. here. He will see you on Monday and make all the necessary arrangements. Now what about some food?"

I went to bed that night with a temperature of 103. Because I have had so much malaria in my life I took a large dose of quinine, but actually I was not at all worried about my physical self. I am physically very strong; indeed, would

not have survived many of the things that have happened
to me had I not been. I now had no doubt but that the
fever would pass and leave my strength unimpaired. In
fact, I only mention it because it seemed to me to have
another bearing on my journey.

I have had fevers of many kinds in all sorts of places and
circumstances, and I believe I can now tell when their
origin is purely physical, and when it is not. Although I
took quinine I was certain that my fever, this time, had no
direct physical cause.

To me, one of the most striking things about fevers is
their mysterious connection with our sense of time and
space. It is almost as if one incorporates within one's own
individual being all the time that has been and can ever be,
and that fever is either the vehicle itself, or evidence of the
means by which one is forced from one time context into
another. The moment one's temperature changes from
normal, one's self ceases to be contemporary. Before now I
have emerged from serious illness with the conviction of
having been in a time and a self anterior to the present,
and the feeling has persisted despite my failure to analyse
or define it. So I have come to believe that, in its most profound sense, our battle for survival is fought out at a level
and in a spirit of which we have little conscious understanding. And what is particularly moving is that, when
the battle is at its grimmest, all those rejected states of life
from slime to tree-fern, from amœba to dinosaur, are
thrown in to preserve the very thing that had found them
wanting.

I think it is the submerged recollection of this great
service, so selflessly rendered by less privileged forms of
life, which gives the sick, on their journey back to normal-
ity, such a keen sense of having shared the mystery of all
living things. It is from the heart of some such recollection
that the world appears rounded and electric with meaning.
The memory is like a sea beside which the reviving spirit
walks, and from which it draws the grateful tears that fill

convalescent eyes at the first sight of a bee tumbling a flower for honey, or a poplar trembling with delicious apprehension under the touch of a June breeze.

Heaven knows I do not want to confuse an experience which is already far enough beyond the reach of words, but I would be running away from what the journey meant to me did I not stress that in this place and time, or wherever it is that one goes with one's fever, it is almost as if the past, the present and the future move so close to one another that they become one. The past, truly recaptured, is time-future coming alive; time-present is a bridge between.

All I would suggest is that the future had begun to register a new design in my blood, and that the fever marked the beginning of its struggle for awareness.

# Chapter Ten

THE following morning I felt most unwell but noticed that the sense of urgency which had come to me at the Club was keener than ever. I therefore got up early and went dutifully through the programme I had set myself and was grateful, as the day went on, to feel the fever ebb from my blood.

I paid my official calls, wrote my name in a book like a Stuart Bible at the gates of Government House, and was able to set off with a light and eager heart to see Martin Boyd, the District Commissioner at Mlanje.

The car was driven by a huge African who called himself Alexander Dougherty-Jackson Btahat-Labambekulu but who wisely asked me to use Jackson only. He drove with an ecstatic expression on his face, and obviously liked to keep moving. When we came over the hills at Limbe and I caught my first view of Mlanje, I told him to stop. He looked really hurt by the order. But one must stop when one sees Mlanje for the first time. I would always stop. It is one of the great views of Africa. Arbuthnot had not exaggerated when he called it "terrific, grand, wizard". On this Monday morning it was particularly impressive.

There was not a cloud in the sky, and I saw it so clearly and distinctly, and in such detail, that it was difficult to believe that it was forty and not ten miles away. Between me and it there lay an immense, flat, featureless plain, burnt black, brown and gold by the sun; its trees and folds curled, withered, twisted, shimmered by heat and drought. Out of it all, Mlanje rose sheer. It stood up straight like a wall for six thousand feet, receded within itself a bit, and then soared sheer again for another three or four thousand feet. Twenty miles and more of it faced me across that immense trembling plain, and I could see nowhere a break or gap which might suggest a possible way up. In that morning sun, it was dark blue, purple and gold, with a most refined, Schiaparelli-like stole of mist round the shoulders of its highest peak.

"Is the Bwana going to go up Mlanje?" Jackson asked me.

"Yes!" I said.

"Auck!" he said, and began to shake with laughter.

"Why do you laugh, Jackson," I asked, "and what does this 'Auck' mean?"

But he only laughed all the more, until I too was affected by it.

As we came nearer the mountain, it became greener and less blue. It was obviously well watered. A deep, dark gorge covered with dense forest, and ending abruptly against a two-thousand-foot cliff, came into view. The innermost peaks disappeared. We crossed a stream or two filled with clear mountain water, but the plain stayed with us. It was amazing how abruptly, like the walls of a Byzantine fortress, the mountain rose out of it.

Then we found ourselves driving through some big tea plantations, mingling the smug green of India and Assam with the shrill metallic hue of Africa. Within an hour and a half of leaving Blantyre, we stopped outside Martin Boyd's boma. We recognized it by the flagstaff and Union Jack flying over it. Both the building and flag looked rather insignificant and forlorn against the huge bulk of the mountain. Its perpendicular grey walls, glistening with water and splashed with moss, entirely dominated the plantations, buildings, and strips of luscious green at its foot.

I myself have always understood perfectly why people who live permanently among mountains find it necessary to endow them with personalities and give them human, if not Christian names. This mountain had, at that moment, a great, grey, compelling Jurassic sort of personality, a character of ill-suppressed rage, a petrified brontosaurus-like grinding and gnashing of teeth, that made everything near it shrink and cower; it presented itself to my senses as a giant striding through time with the plain, like a mongrel, at its heels. I wished I knew what "Mlanje" meant.

Boyd, unfortunately, couldn't tell me, but in every other way he was most helpful. He received me charmingly, and what is more, helped me intelligently and with great good grace.

He had never been up the mountain himself, he said. It had never been possible. He asked me to look at the bumf on his desk, making a despairing gesture. How often I was to see that gesture in Nyasaland; how well I knew it all over Africa! Boyd had one of the largest, the most thickly populated districts in the country.

"I should be out among the people now," he said. "I should be among them all the time. But I can't for this bloody, this pointless bumf, that Zomba sends us. I have not time for essentials, let alone climbing mountains."

He promised that by Thursday, even if he had to empty his jail, he would get me twenty carriers to go up the mountain for a fortnight. It would be difficult, but it would be done. He promised to lend me his own tent and to get me a good personal boy and cook. He promised to write a letter to Dicky Vance, the forestry officer most concerned with the mountain; he had an idea that at the moment Vance, his young wife and a two-months baby, were up the forestry end of the mountain. But he would locate them and ask Vance to help.

Then he looked at me, just as Arbuthnot had done, and said: "Vance is dead keen about trees, you know. He is a bit of a fanatic about forests and this mountain is all the world to him. But I think you will like him."

Again I felt I had been warned, but thought it better not to pursue the subject.

Boyd then took me off to his house, for a four-course

meal. I was continually being astonished at how well people
fed in Nyasaland; at the good wines and sherries that
accompanied the courses.

Suddenly, in the middle of lunch, the clouds came down
and it started to rain violently.

"You want to watch that on the mountain," said Boyd,
"the weather changes in a flash. You know, there is another ruddy great hill over there forty miles away in Portuguese East, called Mount Chiperone. When the wind
gets up, as it does in a second, it brings heavy weather,
usually in multiples of five days. We call them Chiperones,
and they can be the devil. For God's sake, look out for
them up there on that peak."

I was to have tragic reason for remembering that remark, but actually, at the time, I did little more than register it lightly in my mind. I was more interested in the constant references to the forestry officer's love of the trees on
Mlanje which kept reappearing in my official talks. As I
drove away from the Boyds it occurred to me to go and call
on Quillan, the Chief Forestry Officer for the Province.
Near Limbe again I stopped the car on the same neck of
hill on the edge of the plain; but how different now was the
view of the mountain.

Black clouds from the Portuguese border were rolling
over the base of Mlanje and soaring up like deep volcanic
explosions round its flanks. The highest peak had spiked
one of the darkest clouds and seemed to be whirling it
triumphantly round its head; but, as I watched, a whole
concentration of cloud rolled down on it and hid it from
view. I then noticed a very curious thing: the clouds
advanced no farther over the mountain. They had in
their possession one half of it, including the highest peak,
and they seemed content to stay and consolidate their formidable position. But the eastern half of the mountain
remained astonishingly clear and, as the afternoon
deepened, drew lovely colours and tones into its keeping.
It made the mountain appear divided against itself; one

half of it dark and turbulent; the other bending a shining head over the evening.

The incorrigible Jackson, seeing me stare at Mlanje with a kind of hypnotized expression, was inspired once more to ask:

"Bwana! You really going up Mlanje?"

Again I said "Yes" and again he laughed as if he had never heard anything funnier. He was still laughing as we drove on.

Quillan was not at home, and when we were back again in Blantyre I said to Alan: "What is it about your forestry people that I should know? I have a feeling that I am being tactfully warned that my being here is not welcome to them." I went on to explain in detail how that feeling had first arisen in my talk to Arbuthnot on Saturday and seemed confirmed by Boyd to-day.

He told me to worry "nae bit" and rather generously and reassuringly said that I and the forestry "lads" had only to meet and all dangers of complications would vanish. But the fact is: Nyasaland is very small. In it there are no confidences in the real sense of the word, only misleading half-confidences. Everybody knew I was coming and had their own versions about my object in coming. Alan thought the forestry officers were afraid I would either try and take Mlanje away from them or else make their plans for expansion on the mountain impossible.

"But I have not seen it until to-day, so how could I?" I exclaimed. "I have no ideas at all about the place."

Yes, he knew that, but there it was. Quillan and Vance were extremely good "laddies", but he thought something like that might be at the back of their minds. They were rather fanatical about Mlanje and, of course, I knew what foresters were!

"People, obviously, who can't see the wood for the trees," I interrupted with some vehemence, because I hate prejudgment.

Alan burst out laughing and I had to join in.

"But seriously," he said, "why don't you go and talk to Quillan? He is the senior bloke."

I told him I had already called at his office on the way back from Mlanje that afternoon but had found him out.

"I am not surprised. He hates offices," Alan said. "He is out as much as he can because he really loves his trees and his work."

I did see Quillan, however, early the next morning. I was so determined to catch him this time that I beat him to his office, and, as Alan had prophesied, the meeting went well. I took a liking to him at once. It is not difficult to like people provided they have something in their lives that they themselves like. Liking begets liking. The difficult people are the great critics, the ones who cannot find anything in life to like.

Peter Quillan was not in the least of this sort. He was a big, strong, open-air fellow who enjoyed his work, who loved the country and, as I discovered afterwards, had a family to which he was devoted. But he was not free of suspicion of me.

There was one awkward moment, and that right at the beginning when he said brusquely to me: "Before we start, I had better say that I hope you realize the whole of Mlanje is ours and that we intend making it the finest forestry reserve in the country."

I said firmly that I realized nothing of the sort and that it was no concern of mine to realize it. My instructions were to give Mlanje a thorough look-over and, as his department was deeply interested in it—appeared, in fact, to be the only one that had ever done anything about it—I had hoped I would have their expert advice, if not their help and blessing. I had no preconceived ideas about the mountain myself. I had never seen it, and the only plan I had was to go and live with the mountain for a while and let its nature impose its own plan, if any, on me. Besides, although I was not a forester, I was pretty keen about trees myself; not only did I like them and thought the world and

Africa should have many more of them, but I was, in a
sense, profoundly grateful to them. In the war the woods
and jungles of Abyssinia and the East had often, for months,
been my only home.

Thereupon Peter Quillan looked at me, I thought with
some relief, and asked: "Would you mind if I came with
you?"

I said I would be delighted, could not imagine anything
nicer than going over it all together; and it would be the
best way of keeping both ourselves and Mlanje fully in each
other's minds.

Quillan revelled like a schoolboy given an unexpected
half-day's holiday and asked eagerly: "When do we start
and what would you like me to bring with me?"

I asked if Thursday would be too soon and he said: "My
dear chap, I would go right now. I have been itching for
months to lay my hands on that mountain again, and
although I know it as well as anyone, I have never done a
complete round of it. By Jove! we are going to have fun!"

## Chapter Eleven

I LEFT Peter Quillan feeling happier than I had done at any time since leaving London, and went out joyfully to complete my preparations for our expedition to the mountain. There is one thing in Africa that never fails to give me pleasure: getting out of the town into the country, particularly into unknown country. The physical fact of Africa is by far the most exciting and interesting thing about it. The tragedy is that it has not as yet produced the people and the towns worthy of its greatness. By comparison with its physical self everything else looks drab, commonplace and suburban.

It is fun, too, to match one's experience and imagination against the combinations, the enigmatic variations of necessity and circumstance which a journey through Africa can produce. It is rather like playing a game of chess against an opponent of formidable reputation. The opening move determines the end. During the game one uses all the pawns, bishops, knights and queen of one's imagination and initiative. The opponent, however, strikes back not only with mountain, river and lake, rain, wind and all the elements, but also exploits the inevitable distortions in one's innermost pattern, all that tends to accident and disaster inside oneself.

It is a good thing that neither Quillan nor I knew what we were playing against on this occasion, and I, for one, went from shop to shop in Blantyre with nothing but quickening anticipation in my mind.

First of all I ordered boxes to be made that were big enough to hold a forty- to fifty-pound load for each bearer. I then bought food sufficient for a three weeks' journey. Quillan thought we could do it in a week. But, suspicious always of Africa, and considering that neither Quillan nor anyone else had ever made a round trip of the mountain, I trebled the estimate.

I bought some superb hunks of bacon; coils of beef and pork sausages; tins of bully-beef—still the greatest of travellers' standbys—sardines, beans and peas; a bag of potatoes, plenty of rusks and biscuits, sugar, tea, coffee, cocoa, powdered milk, some tins of butter, a tin of marmalade, some tins of green figs and a tin of Cape gooseberry jam. I put in a few surprises for myself and Quillan, and, to make sure that they would be surprises, wrapped them in clean, but ugly, anonymous sacking. I put in two plum-puddings, a two-pound box of assorted chocolates, some dates stuffed with almonds and twenty-eight crisp Jonathans.

I put in a bottle of whisky for my guests and a bottle of cognac for the cold. I bought a good, wide but not too heavy frying-pan, a water-bottle, tin mugs and plates, knives, spoons and forks and a tin-opener, an electric torch, a couple of hurricane lamps, and a large coil of manilla rope. I had my own clasp knife and had borrowed a double-barrelled twelve-bore for which I now bought twenty-five rounds of buck-shot and twenty-five rounds of No. 5 shot. I packed three warm rugs; a trench coat with extra warm lining, a ground sheet, thick socks and stockings, a thick polo-sweater I had had for twenty years; a pair of hob-nailed boots and a pair of stout climbing shoes that had been made in Australia some years before. I took also a prayer-book, Shakespeare, *Modern Love*, and, of course, my sealing-wax.

I bought a small first-aid outfit, some M. & B. and Sulphaguanidine; some quinine for myself and paludrine for the bearers. I was sure the bearers would be full of malaria and that the cold mountain air might bring it on. I even remembered that while I was at Mlanje the doctor had come in to report to Boyd a fatal case of blackwater fever. I bought a couple of bottles of peroxide of hydrogen because nothing convinces an African more that one's medicine is doing his sores good than this harmless disinfectant fizzing on his skin. That is a long way to winning his battle. I also took a large bottle of castor oil, which all Africans love. I went amply prepared.

At dawn on the Thursday morning I said good-bye to Alan. It was raining, and Argyle, much to our amusement, after coming with us to the front door, rubbing his back against my trouser leg for a moment and then putting one sensitive paw carefully on the wet front step, turned round as if he had been stung and scampered back into the house as fast as he could go.

On the way I stopped at the bakery in Limbe. The Greek baker was just taking his bread, lovely crisp, white Mediterranean bread, out of his ovens. The warm, homely smell of bread, charged with the world's oldest civilized memory, in contrast to the tang of the cold rain and damp earth outside, made the sleeping houses around look the most inviting places. I took eight loaves with shining gold crusts into my arms. They warmed me through my bush jacket.

At Limbe I picked up Quillan. He climbed enthusiastically into the car, loaded up with more provisions, bed-rolls, fishing-rods and hurricane lamps. Just after eight o'clock we were at Likabula, the forestry depot at the foot of the mountain, some twelve to fourteen miles from Boyd's boma.

It was drizzling heavily. Only the base of the mountain was visible. But Boyd had been as good as his word. The twenty bearers and a personal boy and cook, a frail, ascetic-looking African, called Leonard among other names, were there waiting for us. They had already divided into loads the tent Boyd was lending me. I noticed with some alarm that it was going to take six men to carry it, and determined to get rid of it as soon as possible. We quickly distributed the remaining loads among them and sent them up the track in front of us. This part of our journey to the forestry depot at Chambe, Quillan said, would not be difficult. They could not go wrong. The difficulties would come later.

I stayed behind with him while he talked to his African officials at the depot. Although I was only a few yards off, a stream from the mountain nearby made such a noise that I could not hear what they were saying. The mist and drizzle swirled thickly round us, but I could feel the presence of the mountain behind it, breathing, as it were, over my shoulder. I hoped it would not be impossible to go up in this weather, but Quillan seemed to have no doubts; said that here he could find his way in the dark.

Just as we were about to start a native runner suddenly came out of the mist down the track towards us, saluted Quillan, and gave him a letter.

"Here!" said Quillan to me: "I think this is for you."

It was a letter from Dicky Vance, written in a large, open, impetuous hand, tilted somewhat backwards as if to put a brake on its obvious impatience.

> "Dear Colonel:
>
> "My wife and I have come up to the forestry depot here at Chambe for some days and look forward to seeing you here. We shall, of course, do all we can to help you, and I have detailed someone to look for you coming over the edge and bring you here. Yours sincerely, R. Vance."

The R. Vance was written quickly, carelessly, as if he did not much like signing his name.

Quillan and I then started our climb. It was easy to begin with and I was grateful, for sitting in ships, trains and aeroplanes had been no training for this kind of thing.

It was still and very quiet; the silence was the true silence of mountains, the silence of the incorruptible and abiding sound of streams, distant waterfalls and casual whiffs of air catching at the leaves of bamboo and tree. Heaven knows what sorts of monstrosities the unpredictable sun of Africa was brewing beyond this mountain of mist and cloud, but on our track we were unaware of its existence.

As the climbing was so easy, we talked as we went, or rather Quillan talked to me backwards over his shoulder as he led the way, turning round and pausing whenever there was a particular point to make. He talked well and had an immense sense of natural detail. He had spent all his adult life in the Colonial forestry service, in Nigeria, Nyasaland, Cyprus and now again Nyasaland. He had worked among all sorts and conditions of forests and trees, but I soon realized that his favourite forests and trees grew in this mountain we were climbing.

It seemed that Mlanje, from the forestry point of view, was unique. There was no other place like it in Africa or the world. It was indeed a world of its own, a very ancient, lost world of trees that grew nowhere else. These trees, he said, had been given the name of cedars, Mlanje cedars, because they looked to the uninitiated eyes like cedar. But they were not cedars at all. They were a conifer of a unique and very ancient sort, had their roots in the most antique of antique African botanical worlds. I would see them for myself soon, in fact I would smell them even before I saw them. Their scent, night and day, filled the air on the mountain; filled it with a heavy, all-pervasive but delicious scent of a lost world; of a time and a place that existed nowhere else.

Their colour, like their scent, was unique. It was green, of course, but like no other green; there was a sheen of the olive green of cypress, and the substance of the green of the ilexes of Greece and the Caucasus; the texture of the conifers of Columbia and the vital electric sparkle of African juniper. In the bark, in the veins and arteries of those trees, the sap, a thick, yellow, resinous sap of a specific gravity and density most unusual in conifers, ran strongly. If you laid your ear to a trunk, it was almost as if you could hear this vital, this dark, secret traffic drumming upwards, skywards, from the deep, ancient soil, the original earth perhaps of Africa, to the outermost, the smallest spike of a leaf, sparkling in the sun a hundred, even a hundred and twenty feet above. So full were the trees of this vital sap that it preserved them even in death; no insect, no worm, no ant would touch even the driest morsel of it. It was the only ant-resisting wood in the whole of Africa.

But when one threw it on the fire, as I would soon see, it was so full of life, of stored-up energy from another world, that it literally exploded into flame. It consumed itself joyfully and gaily, crackling explosively in flame, with none of that lugubrious reluctance to burn of some other woods that Quillan could mention. And fire, unfortunately, had nearly been the cedars' undoing. Some centuries ago, when human beings first appeared in the plains round Mlanje, great fires swept up the mountain and burnt havoc through the responsive cedar woods. They, the Forestry Services, had come just in time to save the remnants of it.

There was still a great deal of forest left—enough for them to exploit in order to get the money to rejuvenate the species, but what I would see was a world of cedars in retreat, a world of unique and irreplaceable living trees, fighting a desperate rearguard action against fire and rapacious human beings, standing-to gallantly, night and day, without cease in the deepest, dampest and remotest recesses of the mountain. Surely I could understand why they were so jealous, so suspicious on the trees' behalf!

In this fashion we climbed for an hour. I remember I had just taken off a sweater and looked at my watch, when I heard the first yodel. It sounded for all the world as if it might have been in the Austrian Tyrol or any of the mountain slopes of Switzerland, and I asked Quillan if there was another party of Europeans ahead of us.

" Oh! no," he said, with a laugh. "Europeans don't come here if they can help it. These are departmental native bearers coming down with sawn cedar from above. They always call like that to one another, particularly when it is misty. You will soon see them. But it is a funny thing about mountains, they always make everyone want to yodel. We didn't teach these blokes. It is their own idea. It just came to them; a gift from the mountain."

He explained that they were so short of good wood in Nyasaland that they were cutting cedar at Chambe, sawing it up by hand and carrying it down the mountain, each length separately on the head of black porters.

"It is hell for them," said Quillan, "but they don't mind and we have got to do it. We make it up to them by feeding them and paying them as well as we can, but we don't like it. We intend changing it as soon as Vance finishes his road on top. At the moment we get more carriers than we can use, because there's a semi-famine on and they want the food."

Just then another yodel soared up like a bird close by. I became aware of a strange, thick, resinous, spiced, oily scent, and Quillan said: "Do you mind getting off the track, please."

There seemed to be a deep sheer drop on our right, so using saplings we pulled ourselves up on to a steep slope to the left of the track. I heard the pad-pad of heavily burdened feet coming out of the mist above, then someone breathing and puffing with every cell of his lungs, followed by a smell of human sweat mingling with the scent of resin, and a native balancing a heavy, thirty-foot beam of cedar on his head, came out of the mist towards us.

I thought it wrong, somehow, that, laden and breathing as he was, he should feel compelled to raise his hand and say, "Morning, Bwana!" Besides, he was just on the edge of a precipice.

"He gets ninepence a day and some food for doing that," said Quillan. "I'd be damned if I'd do it."

From now on we passed dozens of carriers coming down the mountain at regular intervals. Quillan always took the same punctilious care to make way for them. We began to talk less. The track became steeper and we had to use our hands as well as our feet in places. One bit of it passed over a tremendous drop of smooth sheet rock, cyanite I think Quillan called it. The rock had a seventy-degree slope above us, but below it dropped sheer into the mist. We clambered across it from one precarious foothold of moss and aloe root to another.

At half-past ten we stopped to eat a bar of chocolate each. It was much colder, and I put on my sweater. The mist was thicker and blacker, had an English November look about it. At twelve exactly, three hours after our start, as we were going up a particularly steep part of the mountain, using our hands as well as feet in places, I heard dogs barking in the mist above us.

"Those are Vance's dogs. I expect he is coming to meet you," Quillan said, paused, and sniffing at the mist, added: "Do you notice something?"

It was that heavy scent. Every time the timber-carriers went by I had smelt it, a scent that I had not come across anywhere else. But now it was much more confident and pronounced. I nodded.

"Cedars," he said, breathing the scent in with deep satisfaction. "Cedars, as I told you. We are near to the top now."

He had hardly finished his sentence, when two vivid, streamlined, young ridge-back bitches came bounding out of a black cloud at us, gave one leap and a lick at Quillan—how they did it I do not know, because it was all I could do to stand upright there—and bounded back into their cloud again.

I heard the crunch of what sounded like heavy army boots, coming nearer.

A young man wearing an old King's African Rifles' slouch hat, a khaki pullover, officer's pattern, khaki shorts, thick stockings and boots appeared. He was not tall but built rather like the born mountaineer; medium height, broad shoulders, and sturdy legs. He had a frank, open face, grey eyes, rather hidden behind thick glasses, a prominent nose and a chin which looked as if it had been fashioned by experience rather than by an inclination to express determination. He had a deep, firm voice, entirely of a piece with his build.

Quillan introduced us rather as if we were meeting in a drawing-room and not six thousand feet up in the clouds.

"You have struck it unlucky. It's odd, the mountain doing this to-day," Vance said, not without the faintest tinge of something accusing in his tone, as if I were responsible for the change. "I don't know why Mlanje should do this to you. It has been fine here at Chambe up to now. Come on up to the house!"

"Up to the house" I found was another twenty minutes' climb and then a three-mile walk. But I enjoyed every moment of it. Vance and Quillan went ahead, talking the business of the mountain. I followed behind. When we got over the edge, it was half-past twelve, with the invisible sun at its strongest, and the mist lifted to about a thousand feet above us. The peaks were still covered, but the valley, the so-called Chambe plateau up which we had walked, became more and more open to view. I could see at once what Arbuthnot meant by saying it was like a glen in Scotland. It was utterly unlike the Africa we had left down below.

It was covered in lovely long rye, oat and barley grasses, gold-green and purple in their early winter colours. Through the valley on all sides, from behind folds, hills, and many slow gradual rises in its contours, flowed crystal-clear streams, presumably the rainbow trout-streams of which I had heard so much.

At first I thought there were palm trees growing on the banks of the streams, but I soon realized that they were huge tree-ferns, the last remnants of the great cedar forests that once had covered this valley too. The scent of the cedars themselves now was most marked. Soon I began to see them, as Quillan had so vividly described them to me: at first, in small clusters driven back into odd, remote nooks of the valley, but then, as we went deeper into the valley, there appeared in the central gash of it a real, dank, brooding, resentful forest of them. It was rather an awe-inspiring sight. They looked, in an odd way, prehistoric; lovely, but long before human time. I would not have been surprised to see a pterodactyl fly out of them. All round the edges their branches were festooned and heavily hung with long garlands and veils of lichen and moss.

"Aren't they wonderful!" Vance said to me in his clear, firm voice, proudly, as if he had invented them.

He showed me the road he was making from the forest to the edge of the plateau in order to eliminate all heavy manhandling of timber.

"I slept with those blokes under the same blankets," he said, pointing at some black carriers going by bowed down with timber on their heads. "And I like them and hate to see them doing this."

"When? In the war?" I asked.

"Yes. Many a time in Burma," he answered. "I was with the West African Division, Nyasaland battalion, of the King's African Rifles. Arakan! Grand chaps."

"This is very beautiful, well-nigh perfect. Might be somewhere in Europe," I said, realizing it was a half-truth but not yet aware of the full one.

"Yes," he said, with a warm look that took in the whole valley. "Yes. It is absolutely perfect."

Quillan called us over to him. He was standing on a bridge which Vance had built in seasoned cedar of a lovely, Pacific pearl-grey colour.

"Why have you put these beams so far apart?" he asked Vance.

"To save the cedar," Vance said.

"Well, I think that is a bit unnecessary," Quillan said, not unkindly. "Spoiling the ship for a ha'penny-worth of tar. It will bump so when you get your tractor up here."

Vance's face did not change its expression. Yet one knew, in that mysterious way in which changes in the internal atmosphere of human beings make themselves felt, that the remark had hurt him out of all proportion to its context and tone.

"I will alter it if you like," he answered in a level, even voice. "I was trying to save cedars, that's all. But I will change it if you like."

Vance had taken off his hat as he spoke, and the light, cold air of the valley flicked at his fair hair. He looked suddenly fantastically young and hurt; far too young for the grey, old, pre-human world about us. It was almost as if I could see his grown-up mind reach far down inside himself, kneel and attend to the injury of some small lost boy. That done, it stood up, his adult chin took on its determined slant and he said again in that same suspiciously even tone, "I will change it if you like!"

"Oh! Good heavens, no! I was thinking of the future. I wouldn't do it again, though, if I were you," Quillan replied.

"Well! Shall we get along, then?" said Vance, looking past us at the farthest clump of cedars. "I think the mist will be down on us again soon."

I do not think Quillan was at all aware of what his remark had done, and he strode cheerfully on with the incident presumably erased from his mind.

But somehow I felt again as if the incident might be a kind of warning. It linked itself without conscious help from me with those veiled hints of Boyd and Arbuthnot. I felt that the mountain meant more to Vance than even Quillan, much less I, understood at that moment. I had a disconcerting feeling that my mere presence there was an intrusion in someone's most private and intimate world, and that Quillan and I were not walking along a freshly-made road on a wild mountain in Africa, but treading the edges, the actual matter of another human being's dream. And I found myself wishing suddenly that I had not had to come, and my heart went heavy with foreboding.

By the time we had inspected the road and admired the view it was close on three o'clock, and we were all glad to make a bee-line for the forestry hut.

It stood on a high grass-gold mound in the central gash of the valley. There was a wide, clear stream, and a darker fringe of immense cedars round the bottom of the mound. As we made our way slowly towards it, the afternoon light turned it purple, and it looked rather like some kind of un-adorned velvet set in a crown of be-metalled cedars. On either side of the stream there were long slopes of golden grass, speeding away and up to where, three miles farther on, perpendiculars of solid grey cliffs, smooth and shining like the bark of a blue-gum tree, rose two to three thousand feet above the floor of the valley. All round the cliff-tops the mist continued to sag heavily.

The hut itself was built of crossed-cedar beams, lath and plaster. It had a roof of cedar shingles, a little cedar veranda at the back, cedar floor-boards, and, I was to find, a few pieces of crude cedar furniture as well. It burned cedar logs whose flame and smoke added to the cold air their own variants of the generic, all-pervasive scent. The smoke rose straight up for some hundreds of feet, wavered, and then curved slowly back on its course, until it looked like a feathery question mark stuck into the roof of the hut.

"What do you think of it?" Vance asked, pointing a proud possessive finger.

"I must congratulate you on having the only genuine Tudor building I have seen in Africa. It looks charming and absolutely right," I said, and was delighted to hear laughter break through in him again.

"By gosh!" he said. "You're right. It is a bit Ye Olde Hutte-ish; I must tell Val."

His wife, Valerie Vance, "Val" as he and Quillan both called her, had just fed her two-months-old baby Penelope when we arrived. The child was in a wicker basket asleep on the table by the fire whose light flickered over a puckered little face with tightly clenched eyes. The room was in a sort of twilight, warm and gay with the flame and explosive splutter of the burning cedar logs.

As we walked into it the warmth of it set my ears and face

tingling. It was both dining-room and kitchen—there was only one other room in the hut. Val herself just then was cooking a meal for us over a large open hearth.

As she came to meet us, flushed with the heat of the fire, I thought how very young she looked, little more in fact than an attractive, vivacious schoolgirl. As she held her hand out to me the light from the door behind me fell full on her. She had the clear eyes and skin of someone who looked as if she had never lived anywhere else except in the hills. She seemed a deeply contented and happy person, but gave me her hand shyly and, I fear, with some apprehensive reservations that I couldn't fathom. Her greeting of Quillan was more confident but completely impersonal.

"You will forgive me," she said, in a pleasant, matter-of-fact tone, "if I go on with the cooking. Dicky's had nothing to eat since dawn, and you too must be hungry."

"Can't you two get a servant to cook for you, Val?" said Quillan. "It is much too much for you. If you can't, I'll see that you get one at once."

Val stood up from the fire and turned round to give him a slow, shy but determined look, full of meaning, and said:

"I do not want a servant, thank you. Dicky has brought me several, but I don't want them. I do not like anybody cooking for my husband and my child except myself. I do not want anyone even to come in and sweep and make our beds. I want to do it myself. It is just perfect as it is."

"That is quite true," Vance commented, as if underlining a basic law of life. "She doesn't like anybody else in the house."

Again that sickening sense of intrusion, but what could I do about it?

Although they pressed me politely to pitch a bed with Quillan in the room with the fire, I refused. As soon as we had some food, I went and pitched my tent on a level patch of grass about seventy-five yards from the hut and made myself as independent and self-contained as possible. But they insisted on my eating in the hut, and I had to compromise by getting them to take over some of my supplies.

That evening the mist left us. It was apparently a pure product of the sun, of the evaporation that the immense heat causes in the great plains below and its condensation in the cool air round Mlanje's peaks. But the moment the sun went, the mist scurried after it. And it was cold.

We all sat close round the fire and watched those lovely cedar logs burning with an eagerness that belonged to the world when it was yet young. Round about nine o'clock it began to freeze and the fire leapt with the same sort of little independent, purple flames which make farmers in the winter in England exclaim: "My word! Look at that fire! It's going to freeze to-night."

We, or at least Quillan and Vance, talked about trees and forests and their problems, and Val and I listened. I was happy not to speak because I was tired. I preferred to listen and to watch.

Those two children, for so I thought of them, interested me enormously. I had never seen two human beings more complementary, more sufficient unto themselves than those two. She hardly ever took her eyes off him, except now and then to look at Quillan or me to see what effect her husband's remarks were having on us. He frequently would refer to her for confirmation, would stop half-way through a statement and say: "Isn't that so, Val?" or "You noticed it too, Val!" and so on. They never seemed to cease for a second being aware of each other.

When I got up at ten and said "Good-night", Vance came some of the way to the tent with me. The sky was intensely black; pure black, if there is such a thing. The stars were unusually large and clear: so full of light that they seemed to be spilling it over pointed rims, as Vance would have it, "buckets-full at a time".

The night crackled and vibrated with their being; throbbed as it were with an urgent message, a quick, excited, electric, morse-code of stars.

"It looks," I said to Vance, "as if your stars up here burn cedar logs as well."

"By Jove," he said with a deep laugh: "I wouldn't be surprised if they do. Never thought of it. I must tell Val."

I could see, now that my eyes were used to the night, the dark outline of the peaks three miles away. They looked much nearer. How cold it was! I felt Vance shivering near me.

"I think you ought to go back now," I said to him. "It's much too cold and I am nearly there. Look!"

I pointed to where my tent, faintly illuminated by a hurricane lamp, was beginning to show up in the dark.

" Yes: I think I had better, but . . ." Vance began and paused. His teeth were now chattering. I was shivering myself.

"Yes?" I said, turning round to face him.

"I hope you won't mind my saying this," he resumed with an impetuous diffidence. "I hope you won't mind, but look, you are not going to take all this away from us, are you?"

"How could I? And why should I?" I said.

"I don't know," he said miserably. "I don't know, but the feeling seems to be that you might want to use Mlanje for something other than forestry?"

I reassured him as best I could. I said I had not seen Mlanje, had no preconceived notions about it, but judging only from what I had seen that day, it seemed obvious that whatever happened very special provisions would have to be made for the cedars and their rejuvenation. But it seemed to be a tremendous mountain and there might be room for other things besides cedars.

"It is big enough," he said sadly. "It's big enough! That's the trouble. But you know, anything else, particularly sheep or cows, would spoil it. They wouldn't belong. It should all be re-covered with cedars from end to end, as it once was."

I could almost see the earnestness on his face in the dark, and I was moved more than I can say by his concern. I put my hand on his shoulder.

"Don't let us take any fences before we get to them," I suggested as gently as I could. "I am sure it will be all right. We'll see that your cedars are all right, anyway. Now you had better get back. It is too cold for you here. Your teeth are chattering like a monkey's. Good night, and please don't worry."

I waited and shone my torch along the track for him until he was back in the hut. I don't know why, but I watched his sturdy, mountaineer figure disappear into the hut with some misgivings. Again I wondered why, ever since I had first discussed Mlanje in Nyasaland, sooner or later some form of misgiving always arose.

As I stood there, I thought I heard a leopard cough in the cedars nearby. The mountain was full of them, Vance had said. That is why he locked up his two ridge-back bitches every night. There it was again, a startled, excited, almost involuntary expulsion of breath. It was unmistakable, and I loved it. It is one of the most exciting noises I know. I shone my torch along the edges of the cedar copse. I shone it all round the sturdy trunks and all over their patient, aspiring sides, up to their proud, brooding heads. I saw nothing and heard nothing, until the light of my torch near the top of one tree disturbed a bird of sorts, which flew up silently on exaggerated wings like a moth in candle-light. But the leopard, I am sure, was there, watching the night with jewelled eyes. I heard the dogs whimpering from the hut; they were uneasy too. Then came Vance's deep: "Quiet! Lie down, you two. Lie down!"

I went into my tent, drew the flaps round, fastened them tightly, went to bed, and was sung to sleep by the music of new heights in my blood, the rippling of starlight and crackling of frost on the roof overhead.

E

# Chapter Twelve

I spent the following day, Friday, exploring the valley round the hut. There were about twelve square miles in all and I enjoyed myself thoroughly. I collected samples of grasses, of soils, of plants, and had such a busy and interesting day that the time flew by. I got back to the hut after sunset, to find them all round the fire, drinking great big cups of steaming, hot tea. I thought both Vance and his wife looked less apprehensive and their welcome was somewhat warmer.

"Vance," said Quillan, "is coming with us."

"That's grand," I answered, turning to Vance. "But surely we can't leave your wife and baby here alone?"

"Of course he can," said Val quickly for him. "He has never done a complete tour of the mountain. He should do it. It is his job, you know, and he will love it. It is a grand opportunity. If it were not for Penelope, I would come too."

And she would have done. She had been with her husband on all his tours of the mountain.

But I was not happy about it. I did not and I do not trust Africa all that much, and I said so. But they were all three against me. Vance wanted to wait till Monday, when his foresters came back for duty from their week-end in the plain below, and then we would set out on our big tour and make a complete circuit of the mountain.

Meanwhile, on the Saturday and Sunday, Quillan and I took a look at all the outlying eccentric parts of the mountain that would not come into our main circuit. We went and had a look at the biggest of the mountain plateaux, Luchenya, the place where an old lady, "eccentric only in the Nyasaland sense", had once kept cows.

We set off at seven-thirty in the morning, climbed steadily out of our valley and along a ridge which brought us, about two hours later, to a narrow saddle connecting Chambe to the main Mlanje system. It was not difficult climbing, but there was one unpleasant place in the saddle where we climbed over smooth, sheet rock and had a sheer drop of thousands of feet below us.

It was at just this stop, Vance had told me, that once, on her first exploration of the mountain, Val had felt suddenly overcome by exhaustion. What made her aware of her fatigue just at that particular moment she would never know, but the impulse to sit down at once was so compelling and urgent that she had to obey. It was thick with mist and rain. She could hardly see her own feet, but as she sat down a rush of wind from the cold peaks above tore the mist apart and she was horrified to see only two steps away on her track this sudden, this sly drop of thousands of feet.

The rest of the saddle was easy walking, but it was barely a yard wide; a razor-back, with five-thousand-foot drops on either side of it, connecting gigantic peaks. Our excursion across it this Saturday was largely spoilt by mist. Luchenya was a good deal higher than Chambe and therefore much more favoured by cloud. Yet we collected some lovely wild flowers in all sorts of sheltered dells and valleys. Quillan and I came back with armfuls of them; white, scarlet, orange and purple gladiolus; lovely snow-white bell heather; deep purple lobelias.

Two memories of that walk back through the mist remain always with me.

The first: how dark, militant, how resentful was the shade in those remote cedar groves through which we had to go. As one's eyes got used to that dim light, one saw everywhere the raw, bleeding, red, ragged places in their bark where the leopards came daily to sharpen their claws.

The other: our view of Chambe as we came out of the mist over the ridge just before sundown. In that light Chambe, with its deep bowl of a valley, looked like the great bell of a wrecked ship cast upside down on a remote foreshore of time, and like a bell it gathered all its own sounds and silences together and hurled them backwards and forwards from one grey side to another in a steadily ascending spiral to the sky, until, from the rim on which we stood, they were so magnified and reinforced that they seemed to have lost nothing by the great distance they had come.

Suddenly both Quillan and I heard voices, European voices. Although we could distinguish no words, the conversation sounded so close that we stopped and looked round us. At first we could see nothing, but the voices went on in a tone and a manner that suggested a happy, untroubled domestic Saturday afternoon conversation. I could hardly credit my senses, but the voices were those of the Vances down in the valley, nearly a mile away, at the bridge where Quillan some days before had criticized the spacing between the beams of cedar. Vance had Penelope in his arms and Val was by his side. They stood there talking happily. We could not, of course, distinguish what they were saying, but the steady drone of their conversation, the rhythm of their voices, mingling with the far-off sound of falling and running water, continued to suggest an unblemished and rounded moment in their lives. After a while Val took Vance's arm and slowly they started walking back to the hut, still talking steadily. They looked for all the world as if they were alone in Kensington Gardens on a Saturday afternoon instead of on a wild mountain top in Central Africa. I must admit I thought it a strikingly incongruous sight and I said to Quillan:

"You know, they behave as if Chambe were their own private and personal suburb."

"Yes, I know," he answered, and smiled. "They do look thoroughly at home. You wouldn't think that less than a year ago she had never seen Africa and he only knew it very slightly. She came here straight from a Yorkshire Quaker home. We warned him not to bring a wife as we had no house for them and he would have to start life in a hut. He refused to come without her. I must confess I doubted utterly that good could come of it. But I am glad, I was wrong. It couldn't have been better, as you see yourself. Only this morning Val asked me never to move them anywhere else. When I said we would have to in two years' time when Dicky was promoted, she answered disdainfully, 'Oh that! We do not want to be promoted. Dicky and I have talked it over again and again, and we both want to stay here for ever.' It is rather wonderful, isn't it?"

Indeed, I agreed it was wonderful; and yet I had reservations, not perhaps so much on the Vances' score, as on Africa's unpredictable account. I am at heart too much of a nomad to trust and understand love of just one place, particularly one African place. I am sure one cannot love life enough; but I believe, too, one mustn't confuse love of life with the love of certain things in it. One cannot pick the moment and place as one pleases and say, "Enough! This is all I want. This is how it is henceforth to be." That sort of present betrays past and future. Life is its own journey; presupposes its own change and movement, and one tries to arrest them at one's eternal peril. As I listened to Quillan, I just hoped fervently that this most unsuburban of mountains felt about it all as the Vances did.

"If one lived here long," I told him, "I believe one would have to appease the mountain in some big way. I believe one would have to become a Druid of sorts and build some stone altars and sacrifice live leopards on cedar coals to its spirit."

Quillan roared with laughter and said that often in the forests in the hills of Cyprus he felt if only he could pull the boots off the shepherds he would find that they had not human but goats' feet. And on that note we went down to the hut and the Vances.

On the Sunday, we spent the morning in the main cedar wood of the valley, and in the afternoon went fishing. Quillan caught seven rainbow trout, averaging about a pound apiece. The streams were very clear, and it was so fascinating watching the trout pretending, at first, to be unaware of the fly and then rising to strike with incredible speed, that Quillan and I both forgot the time.

It was the cold that first made me realize how late it was and, looking up, I noticed the sun had just gone and darkness was bounding up from the plains below. We raced the cold and the night back to the hut, but before we started it was a race lost. It was so dark when we arrived at the hut, half-frozen, that the dogs from far-off barked at our hurrying footsteps. The Vances were both in front of an enormous fire drying napkins.

"I am glad to see you were not eaten by leopards," said Vance with a smile.

"Why specially to-night?" asked Quillan.

"Only because one of the foresters coming back this evening says he came face to face with a leopard right in the track through the cedars down there," Vance answered.

"What happened?" I asked.

"The usual thing," Vance said with a deep laugh: "they both fell back on previously prepared positions. In other words, ran like hell."

Triumphantly we handed Val the fish. She gave a small cry of surprise, said "How lovely", and then cooked them the Mlanje way in bacon fat with great streaky rashers and sliced potatoes.

That Sunday evening round the fire seemed a very warm, blessed, friendly evening. Things like fires and food, warmth and a roof over one's head, recover their original force of meaning on those occasions. We all ate too much, drank pints of hot, sweet tea, told one another funny stories and laughed as if we did not have a care in the world. But the night was the coldest we had yet had.

"It's going to settle fine for a spell," Vance said as he saw me out. "Look at Orion. I have never seen the Old Hunter so clear."

# Chapter Thirteen

EARLY the next morning we collected our bearers, thirty in all now, with an old forester as guide, and set off immediately after breakfast. The last thing I did was to give my gun and cartridges to Val Vance because I did not feel happy about us leaving her unarmed. She blushed when I gave it to her, was obviously embarrassed, and took it reluctantly only because I insisted. She then came, the two bitches dancing round her, down to the stream with us.

It was our first really sunny morning. We sent the carriers on ahead with the guide. I took my keys and gave them to Leonard, my cook, telling him to have tea ready for us when we arrived at our camp for the night. We waited until the bearers were all across the stream and well strung out along the steep track on the far side, and then prepared to follow ourselves: Quillan and I and Vance last with his rifle-bearer.

Vance paused to say good-bye to his wife. I expect they were very shy, and in any case they were very young; but without looking or wanting to look, one felt it was not the sort of good-bye they meant it to be, was an awkward, brusque, self-conscious gesture quite unrepresentative of their feelings.

It was none of my business but, suddenly feeling sick at heart, I said to myself: "Dear God, I do hope nothing is going to happen to make those children regret their inadequate good-bye."

I record this knowing well that to anyone reading this in comfort, in cold blood, thousands of miles away, my reaction may seem odd, may even seem suspiciously like wisdom after the event. But I can only repeat truthfully that to my clear recollection these were my apprehensions at eight o'clock on the morning of Monday, May 23, six thousand six hundred feet up in the Chambe valley of the great Mlanje plateau of Nyasaland.

This precisely is how I reacted, and now, looking back, it confirms a suspicion that has grown up over many years out of my own troubles and disastrous mistimings in this mysterious business of living. Without looking for it, against all my training and upbringing, I myself have become increasingly aware of how little our conscious knowing pushes back the frontiers of our unknowing. In the forefront of our century all this parade of our knowledge, this great and glittering collection of demonstrable and ascertainable fact, throws no more light on our aboriginal darkness than one of Vance's bright cedar fires throws on the night round the peaks of Mlanje.

And yet there is a way of knowing which is at once underneath and above consciousness of knowing. There is a way in which the collective knowledge of mankind expresses itself, for the finite individual, through mere daily living: a way in which life itself is sheer knowing. So life is to me, anyway; a mystery in all its essentials, a complete and utter mystery. I accept it even gladly as such because the acceptance keeps me humble, keeps me in my little place; prevents me, as we used to say in the recent war, from being caught too far out of position.

And the future? I have been trained to think of it as something before me, something in the days ahead, and so indeed it obviously is. But there is a sense in which it is also behind us, in which it also is "now". I can only reaffirm that without looking for it or seeking it in any way, without any spiritual or theoretical axe to grind, as Vance said good-bye to his wife, I felt desperately afraid for them. And there, for the moment, I must leave it.

She walked back, lightly, easily up the slope to the hut, the light of the sun gay on her hair, and the two bitches running circles round her, and he followed us up the long steep slope out of the valley.

We climbed slowly up the way Quillan and I had gone on the Saturday. For the first time since our arrival, the whole of Mlanje had emerged into the full light of a clear African winter's day. The view from the top was immense.

We saw Lake Chilwa and across it for more than a hundred miles to a blue range of mountains in Portuguese East Africa. We saw the Zomba plateau, the massive Chirudzulu, the Blantyre hills and, beyond, the elegant purple crest of the Kirk ranges. Then we crossed from Chambe to the main Mlanje side by the same narrow saddle ridge where Val Vance had so narrowly missed disaster, turned our backs on the plains and concentrated on Mlanje itself.

Here we climbed, slowly, up the side of a great, grey peak. I wondered again why Mlanje was ever called a plateau, for it seemed from this exalted position a collection of narrow ledges and valleys, poised on six- to seven-thousand-foot cliffs and dominated by a long succession of monstrous, grey peaks. We climbed for two hours. Our carriers spread and straggled out in the long, slowly, steeply ascending line in front of us.

How they did it with those loads I do not know. Unloaded, it was all I could do to get up. In particular, I was amazed at my cook Leonard, the frail, ascetic-looking African from the malarial plain. With a saucepan, a frying-pan, kettle and bag of flour slung round his shoulders, he clattered and banged his way up as steadily and surely as the rest.

Just underneath the tip of the grey peak, we crossed over a thin shoulder and slowly came down once more on to a narrow ledge stretching for twenty miles in front of us, in the lee of a long line of massive, sheet-rock summits. To amuse ourselves, we tried to give them all names according to the impression they made on us: Nelson's Column; Little Pig With-back-so-bare Peak; Cocking-a-Snook Peak; Beer-barrel Point; The Admiral's Hat; Big-pipe-smoking Sioux Chief; The Flappers' Downfall—because, said Quillan, that peak when it fell, like flappers when they fall, fell a long way and fell for good; and finally the Lion's Heart and the Elephant's Head.

In this manner we crossed deep, swollen river-bends, went through thick cedar groves, walked and climbed continually up and down. At three-thirty, when the sun was just drawing in behind the highest peaks, we came to a forestry hut at a place called Tuchila, about thirteen miles from Chambe.

A very old native forester was in charge there. He was a memorable old gentleman, with beautiful manners and the most serene, resolved expression on his face that I have ever seen. He said that, apart from Vance, we were the third group of Europeans he had welcomed there in thirty years. He lived there entirely alone. He had long given up visiting his descendants in the plain below. They never came to see him. His values were fixed for the last time. According to Vance he hardly bothered about his wages any more. Once in four or five months he would come over to Chambe to collect supplies. For the rest he stayed at Tuchila working in his garden, planting potatoes and being unreservedly content. That old man knew something really worth knowing, and I wished I had some way of showing him the respect I felt for him.

In the early morning he led us up the flank of another grey peak, the Elephant's Head. We climbed straight into a blue sky between brightly-lit candelabra of tremendous, scarlet aloes. We climbed steeply for two hours, and then came out on a precipitous shoulder. Here the old man posed, without self-consciousness of any kind, for his photograph, and then said good-bye with great dignity, his hand raised in a Roman salute above his head. While we were resting with our bearers (who were getting to know us and gradually beginning to talk to us not as white strangers but leaders of their team), we watched the old man go down, without a single backward glance, to his home on the edge of a seven-thousand-foot precipice.

The mountain looked very big and he looked very small, and I thought him unbelievably heroic.

From here we went on into a deep valley, called by the guide the Great Ruo. We nearly walked on top of a klip-springer which was obviously unused to this sort of in-vasion and therefore unprepared. It streaked up the peak with the speed and ease of an electric hare.

We went down into the valley. It was filled with smoke, because Vance's foresters were burning protective fire-breaks round the cedars there. We crossed the far shoulder, climbed down into another, the Sombani, valley, and after six hours' continuous and fast walking and climbing in a hot sun, made our camp in a large cave overlooking the great Fort Lister gap in the southern hills of Nyasaland. The natives called this cave "Rock of the God of Won-ders".

We had climbed and walked in all eighteen miles. It was now bitterly cold and we kept a large fire roaring in the entrance all night. I slipped Leonard the first of my sur-prises, a plum-pudding—to celebrate Empire Day. I was a day late remembering it, but it did not spoil our enjoyment in eating the pudding, blazing with some of Quillan's Portuguese brandy.

The next day we traced our steps along the Sombani valley, crossed down an intersecting valley called Malosa, all presided over by the same colossal, grey, sheet-rock presences. They had brows like elder statesmen and looked profoundly engaged in the patient diplomacy of the ele-ments and time. We were soon to have a demonstration of what could happen when they and the clouds put their heads together. With everyone's approval I christened them here "Les Eminences Grises". They had become so real to us by this time that, as I did so, I had an urge to take off my hat and bow politely to them.

We walked down this wide valley below these grey Solomon heads for some hours. It was the loveliest day we had yet struck and a wide blue stream kept us company for several miles. Its water was a perfect mirror to the sun and the sky. I had never seen the mountain more frank, more open and friendly both with nature and with us. It was for me a very happy morning. I was quite content to walk behind Vance and Quillan, who as usual talked forests, trees and mountains with unfailing zest. We got on very well together, but obviously I could only be on the fringes of their calculations.

Just before noon we climbed the inevitable far shoulder of a peak, crossed over it just underneath a wrinkled, eroded and tightly-clenched old mountain face and came down into another valley called the Little Ruo. Oh, these remote, unpeopled Mlanje valleys on their best behaviour on a sunny day; their surging, flashing streams and devout congregations of dark cedars worshipping at the foot of the great cliffs hard by, moaning a mindless, pre-human hymn of their own! They have to be experienced to be believed.

We raced the sun to the steep western rim of the valley, got there almost as soon as the sun did, and looked down in the long level light of the early evening on another far frontier of Mlanje. Here on the brim of the valley, built of wood and grass against an overhanging rock, was the hut of one of Vance's native fire-watchers.

We stopped to look at it and to get our breath. The fire-watcher was not at home, but the world about him was so entirely his own that he had left his precious bow and five delicately feathered, steel-barbed arrows, leaning nonchalantly against the entrance. At the side was a crude stone trap set and ready with seeds spread for the birds.

Suddenly Vance went and pulled the prop out and at once the stone fell down.

"He'll come back and wonder for days what the devil happened to it," said Vance with a mischievously pleased schoolboy laugh, and Quillan joined in with a perfunctory grin.

It seemed to me not only a thoughtless thing to do but,

unintentionally, a betrayal of the unknown watcher's trust. I felt shocked by it out of all proportion to the importance of the material issue involved. Obviously no great practical harm would be done if the trap were left sprung, but somehow I found the incident impossible to stomach. Something was wrong in our set-up, we were off the true somewhere, if we could behave like that. My reaction had nothing to do with the ethics of the occasion; it was the discord that worried me. It jarred as I believe the first misfire, indicating a fault in some smoothly-running machine, must jar on the ears of an engineer.

I was stepping forward to try and set the trap again when an amazed "I say, look at that!" from Quillan, pulled me up short.

This fire-watcher had one of the world's great views at his doorstep. His hut was at least eight thousand feet above sea-level, and close on seven thousand feet above the plain below. Since the mountain fell away sheer to the plain, the whole of Portuguese East Africa was at his feet. However, what had now raised Quillan's interest was not this superb view but a desperate battle between an eagle and a buzzard carried on in the soft evening light.

When I first saw them they were about a thousand feet above us, locked together, and falling fast. At the point where they had first closed for battle a puff of feathers had exploded in the blue-gold air like a burst of ack-ack fire. They fell from above us, and were nearly level with us, before they disengaged their talons and regained their ruffled wings. Then up they went again, watchfully circling each other. In the cold, mellowing light we stood below, bearers and all, holding our breaths with a curious excitement, as they drove each other up. The buzzard was the first to reach the height it sought. Suddenly it shot up, did a loop, and came down on the eagle once again, beak, talons, wings and all.

There was another burst of feathers as the birds fell. They shot by us at a tremendous speed and then, far below us, the eagle broke free and fled. The buzzard made no effort to pursue it but rose impressively to a tremendous height on one of the great currents from the plain, and then on calm, impassive wings floated away over the grey peaks behind us.

We had neither ideas nor theories as to what the battle had been about, but I am sure of one thing: had we been ancient Greeks, whose manhood would not be dishonoured by tears nor by the pouring out of libations to the gods, then we would have taken a different interest in the encounter. I could almost hear the Homeric rendering: "Just then Zeus, the all-powerful, sent a buzzard to defeat the eagle as a warning to the sorely-tried Odysseus that greater perils lay ahead", and so on. But we had not the mind for such fancies. We had walked and climbed twenty miles. So we pushed on as fast as possible down the far side of the mountain towards our rest, and, for the moment, I forgot all about the fire-watcher and his sprung trap.

Just below us, on one of the spurs which rose up from the plain like a flying buttress supporting the immense, Gothic flank of the mountain, we climbed down on to the thickest and darkest cluster of cedars we had yet seen. The light of the sun struck a cold, steely sparkle from their erect tops. They looked suspicious even of the intentions of a most noble and generous evening. Once among them, it became quite dark. Quillan, Vance and I joined hands and could hardly get our arms half-way round many of the trunks, nor could we see a trace of the blue of evening above.

We had hardly entered the forest when I heard from far away the harsh, grating noise of mechanical saws. It really was a heart-rending sound and shattered that beautifully poised moment of evening-fall with its violent hysteria. Vance and Quillan both looked instantly ashamed of it, and hastened to apologize.

They said they had been unable to prevent it. This part

of the mountain had been taken from their control. The shortage of wood in the country was such that the government had given some Europeans from the plains a concession to cut timber here. The only thing to be said for it was that it produced more money for rejuvenating the species elsewhere in the mountain. But they hated it, and wanted it stopped.

I was convinced, as I listened to those two, that the trees knew what was happening to their kind in that area. The noise was so obviously the voice of destruction, and besides, death was in the very air they breathed through their fine dark leaves. Their characteristic scent, which lay so heavily on the air, here had an extra tang to it—the smell of the sap, the honey-gold essence of freshly felled, warmly carved and still bleeding cedars.

We slept that night in the tiny log hut of the half-caste manager of the concession. No European would face the lonely life on the mountain except at an exorbitant wage; no native was educated and expert enough; so, as often happens in Africa, the half-caste was the inevitable compromise.

This half-caste, however, had an unusual quality about him. He was a tall, good-looking boy with regular, sensitive features and a pair of big, well-spaced dark eyes. His name was Fitz David St. Leger and he had a neat, carefully clipped, cavalry moustache on a quite un-negroid lip. I was told that his father, an ex-officer of the Greys, was still alive in the plain below, living with a black wife and a large brood of chocolate children. He was, everyone said, a man of great charm and distinguished appearance. About twenty years before he had won the Calcutta sweep and tried to begin life afresh in Europe. He had even married a European wife. But no miracle of money could save him from Africa. Within a few months he was back, swearing that he could not endure pale-faces, particularly pale-faced women.

This son of his must have modelled himself on his father

or some other ancestral memory. He seemed an intelligent, capable boy, with something of the cavalry
subaltern in his bearing, but so vulnerable, so hopelessly,
unfairly and basically vulnerable that I could not see him
ever making the most of his qualities in that British-
African world. One imagined him, for the rest of life,
drifting from one weary compromise to another, living a
sort of twilight existence between two worlds.

And he was much nicer to us than we deserved. He
turned out of his hut the moment we arrived. He quickly
had his bedding rolled up, and he told us to use an enormous cast-iron bath that he had brought up the mountain
with him. I tried to get him to stay and eat with us but in
vain. He raised his soiled white topee, bade us a polite,
strangely old-fashioned "good evening" and went off to
spend the night in a hut with his natives.

I think I enjoyed that night less than any of its pre-
decessors. As we sat in our greatcoats, huddled round a
pathetic table made of petrol boxes, our conversation just
missed being tediously argumentative. At times I felt as if
some outside force beyond our immediate awareness was
deliberately trying to set us quarrelling. Also, the hut
stood hard by an enormous pile of golden cedar sawdust,
and the smell of warm cedar sap was so overpowering that
I felt stifled by it. For a long time I couldn't sleep and my
mind tended to return ceaselessly to the trivial discords
of the day.

I was relieved when morning came. One of the first
things I did was to go and thank Fitz David St. Leger for
his hospitality. I was amazed when I held out my hand to
him to see him draw his arm back. He flushed under his
dark skin and said, "I am not clean enough." When we
did finally shake hands, he did it awkwardly as if his own
was burning. Vance and Quillan, I noticed, watched me
with embarrassment and did not follow my example.

# Chapter Fourteen

THEN, on that Friday, May 27, we climbed back on to the highest edge of the Little Ruo valley, about eight thousand five hundred feet high. There Quillan and Vance decided to take a short-cut to our camp for the night and to send our bearers round the long, easy, known route with our guide. They did this because there was some unknown country in front that they thought we should see. As we stood on the rim, talking it over, in a cold breeze and under a grey, morning sky, I noticed far away in the plain below the lumber camp, the top of Mount Chiperone covered in cloud. The wind was blowing off it towards us and the weather was rapidly building up round it.

In a flash I remembered Boyd's warning to me in his house at Mlanje: "For God's sake, when that happens on the peak, look out."

So I said to Quillan and Vance: "It looks to me as if there is a Chiperone on the way. Don't let's take any chances! I don't like short-cuts anyway. My experience of mountains is that the longest way round is the shortest way there."

They turned round, regarded Chiperone solemnly for a moment, looked at each other, nodded, and then Quillan said: "It is only a bit of morning mist. It will clear up soon. We'll be in the camp in an hour or two and can spend the afternoon resting. I think we can all do with it."

Because they were the experts on the mountain, because it was their mountain and their mountain's weather, and because I have been trained to give priority to what appears to be reasonable, I stifled my instinct and said no more. But if the future had an origin other than in itself, then I believe it was born in that moment. Our decision was a bad decision, it was the wrong decision. Wrong begets wrong, starts a chain of accident and disharmony in circumstances which quickly develop a will of their own. These circumstances exact their own logical toll and must run their time to the bitter end, before the individual is able to break free of them again.

We sent our bearers on their way, kept only Vance's own gun-bearer with us, dropped quickly into the valley below, crossed a wide stream and started up on the other side. We climbed hard and fast. It was eleven o'clock exactly when we came out on the rim close on nine thousand feet. We sat down, ate a piece of chocolate and prepared to admire the view.

Almost directly underneath us was the greatest of Mlanje's many dark gorges, the Great Ruo gorge. The water of the Great Ruo river itself plunged down the top end of the gorge; fell with a wild, desperate, foaming leap into an abyss, thousands of feet deep. We could not see the bottom of it. On either side it was flanked by black, glistening, six-thousand-foot cliffs, tapering off into grey peaks nine thousand feet high. The whole of the gorge rustled, whispered and murmured with the sound of falling water, which at every change of mountain air would suddenly break over us with a noise like the sound of an approaching hail-storm.

"You see that clump of cedars just beyond the fall," Vance said; "our camp is there. We shall be there within the hour."

As he spoke the mist came down. He and Quillan said it would soon lift. We waited. We got colder and colder. The mist rapidly thickened. It began to drizzle. At eleven-thirty we decided to do the best we could. The sun had vanished, the wind had dropped. Neither Vance, Quillan, I, nor, for that matter, any living person, had ever stood before where we then stood. In the sunlight one stone is very like another; but in the mist on Mlanje they were undistinguishable. Because of that terrible gorge we could not go farther down until we were past the head of the waterfall. So we set out along the peaks, keeping as near to their crest as we could.

Worst of all, the mist halo lay like a blanket over the noise of the fall. Not a sound came up to us. We had not even a whisper from it for guidance. The silence was really complete, except for our breathing, our boots squelching on the wet grass and moss or crunching on stone.

From eleven-thirty until four-thirty—and we had been going since seven without rest—we went up one peak and down into a bottom, up the other side and down again.

At half-past four the rifle-bearer said: "It is no good, Bwana; we are lost. Let us make a fire and wait for it to clear."

I said no. I knew it was no mist. It was a Chiperone and it came, so Boyd had said, in multiples of five days. We would be dead of cold before it cleared. I added, "At all costs, we must go down now. The night is not far off. We must get into a valley and then we can consider the next step."

So slowly down we went, down those steep, uneven slopes of Mlanje, listening carefully for the noise of falling water. But the whole mountain had gone as silent as the dead.

We slid and slithered in a way that was neither prudent nor safe. Suddenly at five the mist began to thin. The gun-bearer gave a tremendous shout. A warm golden glow was coming up to meet us and in a few minutes we were in the tawny-grass bottom of the Great Ruo itself, three miles above the gorge and four miles from our camp. We got to our camp at nightfall and the mist changed into a heavy, steady, drumming downpour of rain. The bearers were already in and Leonard had prepared our little mud-and-straw native hut. We lay down by the side of the fire in the middle of the hut, a great glow of gratitude inside us. We were too tired to speak for half an hour or more, and listened to the violence of the rain.

"It is a Chiperone all right now," said Vance: "the point is, how long is it going to last?"

Our camp was a disused, discarded lumber camp, the huts which had originally housed the native timber carriers. Once again, as often before in Africa, I thanked Providence for the African hut-builder. These insignificant-looking, brown beehive huts one dashes past by car or train in Africa are amazing. Considering the poor material, the lack of scientific equipment and research, the lack of education of their humble builders, they are works of genius. Although the rain now pounded down so violently, not a drop came through the ancient thatch.

When we had recovered sufficiently, we went round to inquire after our bearers and found them, also under dry roofs, cooking their dinners round crackling cedar fires. They were a happy and cheering sight.

We told Leonard to stay with them in the dry. We did not want him splashing round in the wet, trying to wait on us. We went back, dried ourselves out thoroughly, and did our own cooking. I made a kettleful of hot coffee which we drank very sweet, laced liberally with my medicinal cognac. The cognac was a great improvement on the Portuguese brandy and a welcome and complete surprise. It was precisely the anticipation of moments like these that had made shopping in Blantyre such fun, and I drew a glow of reassurance from this slight justification of my planning.

We ate in silence. I myself was too full of an unutterable sense of well-being to attempt to speak. I think the others perhaps felt something else as well, for they both, particularly Vance, looked somewhat reproved by the experience of the day. Then silently we stretched ourselves out beside the fire, with a good heart, to sleep.

But I was too tired to sleep at once. I lay with my ear

close to the ground and listened to the rain drumming down on the mountain. Among those vast peaks there was no other sound than this continuous, violent downpouring of the rain. There was no light of stars or far-off reflection of town or hamlet; only the dying glow of the cedars from a dying world of trees. The night, the mountain and the rain were woven tightly into a dark pre-human communion of absolute oneness. No leopard, pig or antelope or elastic mountain gazelle would venture out on a night like this. It is precisely against moments like these that the leopards bury some portion of bird, bush ape or pig, and leave it near their holes and caves. The summons riding the mountains with such desperate dispatch was not for animal or human hearts. But it was as if the earth underneath my head was slowly beginning to respond to this drumming, this insistent beat of the rain; to take up this rhythm of the rain; to answer this ceaseless knocking at its most secret door, and to open itself to this vast orchestration of its own natural, primeval elements, to begin to quicken its own patient pulse, and deep inside itself, in the core of its mountain, its Jurassic heart, to do a tap-dance of its own. Whenever I rose in the night to make up the fire there was the rain and this manner of the rain; and when I lay down again there was this deep, rhythmical response of the earth.

We woke finally at five and talked over the day while waiting for the kettle to boil. Our plan originally had been to go over the top of the mountain in the direction of Chambe. But we found now that our experience of the day before among the peaks on the far side of the Ruo valley had made us all decide in the night against any more adventures in the clouds while the Chiperone was blowing. In this way the previous day influenced our behaviour. Our guide well knew the way over the top and, had it not been for that short-cut, I do not believe we would have changed our plans.

Vance now said he knew an easy way down off the

mountain which led to a large tea estate at the bottom. Quillan said he knew it too; it was the old timber-carriers' track. It was steep, but cut out in the side of the Great Ruo gorge and clearly defined. We could not go wrong. Only it meant abandoning the last part of the trip and that, he thought, would be a pity for me. I said firmly, "Abandon." Vance then decided to go ahead to the tea estate and get a truck to take us round by road to Lika-bula. With luck, he said, we could all be back on the mountain at Chambe that evening.

With our last eggs I made him a quick omelette for breakfast, and sent him off in the rain. Quillan and I followed slowly with the carriers.

We set out at eight but the rain was so thick and violent that there was only a dim, first-light around us. We went slowly. The track was steep and highly dangerous. On the left of us, only a yard or so away, was that deep cleft down to the Great Ruo gorge. The bearers too had great difficulty with their loads. They had to lower themselves down from one level to another by cedar roots and help one another down perilous mud precipices.

As we went down, the noise of falling water all round us became deafening. Whenever there was a slight lift of the rain and mist, the half-light, the mepacrine gloom on the mountain would be suddenly illuminated by a broad, vivid flash of foaming white water leaping down the face of smooth black cliffs, thousands of feet high. We had to shout in places to make ourselves heard.

Moreover the mountain itself, the very stones on which we trod, the mud wherein we slid, seemed to begin to vibrate and tremble under this terrible pounding of water. At moments when we rested, the ground shook like a greaser's platform in the engine-room of a great ship. This movement underfoot, combined with the movement of the flashing, leaping, foaming water in our eyes, and driving rain and swirling mists, gave to our world a devastating sense of instability. The farther down we went, the more pronounced it became, until I began to fear that the whole track would suddenly slither like a crocodile from underneath my feet and leave me falling for ever under the rain and Mlanje's cataclysmic water. It needed a conscious effort of will to keep me upright, and I found this all the more difficult because of a new complication that was arising. I began to feel as if my very senses were abandoning their moorings inside myself.

Luckily this stage of the journey did not last too long. Two and a quarter hours later our track suddenly became easier and broader.

Quillan said, "We'll soon be off it now."

We came round a bend in the track and there, to our surprise, was Vance. He was sitting at the side of a fast stream of water which was pouring over the track and had evidently held him up. He was joining some lengths of creeper, of monkey rope, together.

"I didn't want to cross this stream without a rope," he said. "I have been up and down this stream as far as possible and this is the best place to try it. It doesn't look difficult. Do you think this will do?"

He handed me his rope of creepers.

"No! Certainly not," I said, and looked at the stream.

Its beginnings, above us, were lost in the mist and rain. Then it suddenly appeared out of the gloom about a hundred yards above, charging down at us at a steep angle, and finally, just before it reached us, smashing itself up behind a tremendous rock, deeply embedded on the side of the gorge. Somewhere behind the rock it reassembled its shattered self and emerged from behind it flowing smoothly. For about twenty yards it looked a quiet, well-behaved stream but, on our left at the track's edge, it resumed its headlong fall into the terrible main Ruo gorge below us. I now went to this edge and looked over, but the falling water vanished quickly in the gloom and told me nothing. Only the ground shook with the movement as my eyes and head ached with the noise.

I came back and found Quillan lighting a fire.

"Our bearers are nearly dead with cold," he explained. "They'll crack up if we don't do something. Two wood-cutter blokes died here of exposure two years ago. But if I can get this fire going for them in the lee of this rock, our chaps will be all right."

The rain poured down even more heavily than before, and it looked darker than ever. The shivering negroes, the bamboos bent low with rain, the black rocks, were like figures and things moving in the twilight of a dream.

Again I went and looked at the stream above. Vance appeared to have chosen rightly. The stream was swollen but did not look dangerous at that point, particularly with a good rope. Higher up it would have been hopeless.

"I tell you, Dicky," I said. (It was the first time I had called him that and I don't know why I did, except that we all suddenly seemed to be very close to one another.) "I tell you what, Dicky. We'll take all our ropes, you knot them together and then I'll go across. I am bigger than you."

"I don't think that is necessary," he said. "I know the way. You don't. And with a rope it will be easy."

We joined up the ropes, tested the result in every way, pulling it, leaning on it. It seemed tight and strong. We took Vance's valise straps and added them to the end, just in case. I then tied it round Vance's chest with a knot that couldn't slip. I made sure it could not tighten and hinder his breathing.

As I tied it I said, "Dicky, are you sure you are happy about this and know how to do it, for if you are not I would much rather do it myself?"

"Of course I know," he said with a deep laugh. "I have done it scores of times in Burma. And I must hurry. I want to get those poor black devils under shelter as soon as I can."

"Well, remember," I said, "keep your face to the stream; always lean against it; go into it carefully and feel well round your feet with your stick before you move."

He took up the stout stick that we had cut for him. I called Quillan and two of the bearers. Quillan and I took the rope. I braced my feet against a tree on the edge of the stream, just in case, but I was not at all worried.

Vance waded in. The water came about to his navel. He went steadily on for some distance, then, to my bewilderment, turned his back slightly on the stream. It was the first deviation from plan.

He took another step or two, stopped, suddenly abandoned his stick to the stream and yelled to us, "Let out the rope!"

It was the second deviation from plan. I was horrified. What the hell was he up to? Before we had even properly grasped his meaning he had thrown himself on the stream and was swimming a breast-stroke. As was inevitable, the stream at once caught him and quickly swept him to where it foamed and bubbled like a waterfall over the edge of the track. The unexpected speed with which all of this had happened was the most terrifying thing about it. Even so, Vance had got to within a foot of the far bank, was on the verge of reaching it—when the water swept him over the edge and he disappeared from our view.

Quillan and I were braced for the shock. As we saw it coming we both shouted for the bearers, who rushed to our assistance in a body. The rope tightened in a flash. The strain was tremendous. Vance's body, no longer waterborne but suspended out of sight, below the edge of the rocky track, with the weight and stream of water pouring on top of it, strained the rope to the utmost. Yet it held.

I think it would have continued to hold if the angle and violent impact of the water on the body had not now with incredible speed whipped Vance along the sharp edge of the rocks, swung him from the far side over towards our bank and chafed the rope badly in the process. It still held for a second or two. We worked our way along it towards him—were within two yards of him—when the rope snapped.

At that moment we knew that he was dead. Anyone who stood with us in the black rain, amid those black cliffs in that world of storming, falling, rushing, blind water, must have known that he was dead. Quillan turned round, lifted a face to me naked and bare with misery, and said hoarsely, "What to do now? He is dead, you know!"

I nodded and said, "Please take a search-party as far as you can, Peter, and see what you can see."

He immediately set out. I called Leonard and some bearers and started to undo our baggage. It was obvious we could not cross now. We had lost all our rope; we had lost one body with a rope, we could not risk losing one without a rope. Nor could we stay there.

Quillan was back almost at once. I was not surprised. We were, as I have said before, on the edge of the Great Ruo gorge.

He shook his head. "Not a sign, not a hope. He is dead and there is nothing we can do now except to see that these fellows don't conk out."

He indicated the bearers.

We called them all round us. They were cold and terribly shaken by Vance's death. One old man was crying and they were all shivering as if with malaria. We told them to dump their loads and to start back up the mountain to the huts we had slept in the night before. A moan of despair rose up from them. They said they wanted to sit by the river, wanted to make a fire and wait for the sun. But I knew that that only meant that the spirit had gone out of them, that they had given up hope and were resigned to do no more than sit down and die in comfort.

It was then that Leonard, the puny plainsman, the sophisticated native from the towns, stood up, unsolicited, and lashed them with his tongue. I don't know what he said, but he insulted them into some shape of spirit.

We distributed all our own and Vance's clothing among them. That cheered them. They began to laugh and to tease one another, at the sight of their companions in tennis shirts, grey sweaters too big for them, in green, blue, red and grey striped pyjamas, and my own green jungle bush-shirts with their red 15 Corps flashes still on them.

I expect it was an incongruous sight in that world of rain, falling water and black, impersonal rock, but I did not find it at all funny. It seemed to me to fill the cup of our misery to overflowing. I expect whatever gods sit on this African Olympus might well find it amusing to kill a young man of twenty-eight in order to dress up some of the despised, ubiquitous outcasts of their African kingdom in silk pyjamas in the pouring rain. To me, just to kill was bad enough; to mock the kill an intolerable perfection of tragedy. I came near to joining in Quillan's tears at that moment, but fortunately I got angry as well, so angry that I believe if my strength had matched my rage I could have picked up the whole of Mlanje and thrown it over the edge of the world into the pit of time itself.

I walked up to the bearers in anger such as I have never known and told them, by look and gestures, to get the hell up the mountain without delay. In that mood, Quillan and I got them up the steep, slippery sides of the gorge that we had come down only a few moments before.

At half-past twelve we were back in our camp of the night before; we started a great, blazing fire and dried ourselves. The warmth and the sight of fire and smoke effected an amazing revival of spirit among the Africans. I was discussing with Quillan a plan for going out myself through the Fort Lister gap to fetch help, leaving him there with the bearers because he knew the language, when the oldest forester spoke up and said: "You can't do that, Bwana. It is too far. But I know a short way over the top that will bring us to Chambe safely by sundown."

Quillan asked them all if they had heard what the forester said, understood, approved and were prepared to

follow him implicitly?  They all said emphatically, "Yes!"
It was the only thing to do and they would do it.

By one o'clock we were climbing back up the peaks behind our camp, into clouds and into rain which seemed
more violent than ever.

Peter Quillan was at his best.  He was firm yet patient
with the bearers, steadily urged them on, but it could not
have been easy.  He was heart-broken, and from time to
time I could see he was in tears.  He was deeply attached
to Vance and was blaming himself bitterly for the accident.
I did my best to comfort him.  I couldn't see how he was
to be blamed at all, and if he were, then what about me?
He, after all, had not been worried by a sense of the future.
It wasn't he who had lain awake at nights half stifled by a
sense of death and listening to the dark drummer of Africa
beating-up the weather round Mlanje.  But as I com-
forted him and we slowly forced the bearers up the black
peaks in front of us, I too was sick at heart and desperately
tired.

Without any preliminary training I had been scrambling
round these monstrous peaks from dawn until sunset for
nine days, and I could now hardly lift my legs.  Heaven
knows I was fit, my lungs and spirit were all right, and my
rage with the mountain and its gorge spurred me on.  The
problem was purely mechanical.  My legs and feet were so
abused that the muscles rebelled and would not react instinctively.  It seemed to me that all my reflexes had gone.
I had to treat each step as a mechanical and separate
entity in the movement of my body.  I could move only
with a deliberate, calculated, conscious and determined
effort of will.  At one moment I thought seriously of re-
tiring to the huts lest I should not be able to continue, and
so should bring disaster on the others.

Quillan was amazing.  His forester's muscles were intact.  He cheered and helped me on by word and example.
When, afterwards, we told people of this journey over the
highest and wildest part of Mlanje they would hardly

credit it. But on the day of Vance's death we did nearly twenty miles' climbing. I hope never to do such a journey again.

For two hours after leaving the hut we continued to climb, at the steepest of angles, into deepening cloud and rain. Our guide, the old forester, in his rags and tatters, dripping with water, was unbelievable. He climbed at our head with his stick held in one hand in front of him. Every now and then he parted the grasses with it, peered at them intently, or tapped a stone, listening carefully to its ring, and then changed direction to the left or the right; but he never faltered. Over and over again the rain and mist completely hid him from my view. It was dark, it was black; even at the best of times it was grey all around us.

After two hours, as far as one could judge in the mist, we seemed to pass right over the top of a peak, and our course began to drop slowly down. The relief to my muscles was timely.

Quillan offered me some whisky and water. I do not drink spirits as a rule, but I accepted gratefully and pushed on with renewed energy. At four o'clock we suddenly came out of the mist and rain; we walked through it as if it had been a wall. At one minute it was raining; the next we were in the sunlight looking down on the long ledge by Tuchila.

We climbed down there as fast as we could. We had seven miles to go before we reached that razor saddle, and unless we got there before dark we should be unable to cross to Chambe and shelter.

We got down easily enough, but getting up and then down the river gashes and finally up again on to that high steep shoulder by Chambe was for me a bitter and protracted agony. However, we got to the ridge where Val Vance was nearly killed, just as the sun went down.

It was a frightening sunset, a sort of cosmic schism of light and darkness. On our left was that immense, dark pile of rain, turning and wheeling constantly over the bulk of Mlanje, wheeling in such a manner, with such fantastic contortions of cloud shapes, that to my tired eyes it looked as if the devils of death were charging up and down those peaks on phantom, skeleton chargers. Yet to our right lay Chambe with a golden afterglow of sunlight on it, untroubled and serene, as if it had never known death or disaster of any kind. Less than a fortnight before I had seen Mlanje from afar at just such an hour, in such a way with this same pattern of fair and foul, dark and light, on it. Had the same pattern also been in me?

## Chapter Fifteen

THE bearers, climbing for once without loads of any kind, were by this time a long way ahead of us. We had realized this would happen and had warned them not to arrive at Val Vance's hut before we did. We were concerned that their looks would betray our tragedy to her. We now found them waiting for us huddled together silently on the slope above the stream at the bottom of Chambe. The sense of tragedy was back with them too, and as we reached them they crowded silently round Quillan and me, peering anxiously at us. We told them to keep very quiet and fall in behind us.

The first stars were out; the night symphony of Chambe was tuning in.

"Oh! I do hope," Quillan said in great distress, "the dogs won't bark and bring Val out!"

But the dogs did not bark. The hut was deathly quiet, might have appeared deserted if it had not been for a dark plume of cedar-scented smoke on the sky and a flickering glow behind the window. As we walked by it, we saw Val sitting in front of the fire, among Penelope's napkins, her hands in her lap. Framed in that small square window it looked like the subject of a Dutch interior full of warmth, security and domestic calm. She had not, as yet, lit the lamps and was sitting there in the firelight in a dream of her own.

We opened the door. Val jumped up and came towards us with a look of glad surprise and said happily: "Oh! How very nice. Somehow I did not expect Dicky tonight."

On the mountain Quillan had said that he felt he ought to break the news to Val as Vance, after all, was his officer, but this was too much for his shattered heart. He broke down and buried his face in his hand, while the two bitches jumped up round him, licking his neck and head.

So I took Val by the arm and said, "Val, dear! Hold on to me for a minute, and please listen carefully to what I have to say. Dicky is dead. He was killed this morning."

"Oh! no," she said. "Oh, no! Oh, no!"

"Yes, Val," I answered, "he is dead. I am so sorry, so dreadfully sorry, but there is not any possibility of a mistake. He is dead. We saw him killed."

She looked at me and it was as if I saw, far down in her eyes, all their days together go out, one by one, like a series of candles. The image of Dicky, alive, seemed to me to leave her; it was wrenched from her like the topmost leaf torn from a high tree by a fierce blast of wind and sent falling down, vainly fluttering to retain its height, down below for good; down, down, and out of the sunlight of her mind, for ever.

For a moment then, I do believe, she too died as Vance had died, and life, as we normally understood it, stopped abruptly within her. It was as if I was looking right into a heart suddenly emptied of meaning. I saw something rounded and whole suddenly become such sheer, utter and black nothingness that my own pulse missed a beat at the horror of it. And then the tears welled up and spilt. I do not know what I should have done if she had not cried. I thanked God for sending those tears so urgently needed. I thanked God, and as I saw her crying bitterly like a child being born, she too seemed to come alive again. I put her gently in a chair by the fire and let the flames of those ancient cedars, older even than human tears, wrap their antique warmth about her.

That night Quillan and I did not leave her alone for a moment. We put mattresses in front of the fire and made up beds for all three of us. When she ceased crying for a while we talked to her. First, I told Val in detail what had

F

happened, while Quillan dried out our things, for we were wet through and half frozen. He then made some food which no one would eat, saw to it that Val fed Penelope, and himself changed the baby's napkins. Then he came and told Val everything that had happened and I took over the domestic details.

After a while we all lay down by the fire, Val between us. But we none of us slept. We talked to Val incessantly, for the moment we stopped she began to shake with spasms of tearless sobs, as people do when they are really physically too tired for more crying.

The talking helped and she asked us many questions. I told her the truth as I saw it without reserve or qualification. I spared her no details where she asked for them. I respected her questions as carrying the seeds of their own healing, however brutal the answers may have appeared to my reason.

One of the most pathetic things about us human beings is our touching belief that there are times when the truth is not good enough for us; that it can and must be improved upon. We have to be utterly broken before we can realize that it is impossible to better the truth. It is the very truth we deny which so tenderly and forgivingly picks up the fragments and puts them together again. Miserable as I was, I took heart from Val's instinct not to flinch from any aspect of the horror brought about by us and the mountain.

Indeed, so pronounced was this instinct in her that that night she tried to relive with us every aspect of her relationship with Vance. For instance, she turned to me and asked quietly, like a very small girl:

"Did you think Dicky was handsome?"

"No, Val!" I replied. "He was not handsome, in the way most people mean it. But he had a very nice face."

"What do you mean by a nice face?" This was said not impatiently, but with an obvious longing for precision.

"Well, his eyes were big and well spaced." She nodded,

and I went on, "And they had an open, honest, but rather hurt and puzzled expression in them."

"So you noticed that too," she said with a desperate catch at her voice. "You see, he was so hurt as a child. Nobody seemed to care much about him. People looked on him as a failure. They were so horribly patronizing about him. Even here on the mountain tiny things could hurt him terribly. But I was going to make it all right for him. He said already it was so much better. I meant him never to be hurt again"—and she started crying again.

I went on quickly. "Then he had a very good brow, Val, and a broad forehead, and pleasant colouring. His nose and chin were a bit too long and determined to give the whole of his features the regularity that we call hand-some. But the general effect was very pleasant and boy-ishly sympathetic."

"Yes! But you have not mentioned his teeth," she inter-rupted. "They were not really good, and what about his figure?"

"He was not tall enough to be imposing, but he was sturdy, strong and well proportioned, and I liked his voice a lot."

"I don't know if you are altogether right," she said slowly, talking from very far back in time and her mind. "He had rather a funny face and a funny, odd, boyish body. But, do you know, there was not a thing about him, not a hair on his head or a tooth in his mouth that I wanted any different. I loved every bit of him as he was. Oh, Dicky!" and there she was, back in the present, crying bitterly. Presently she stopped and said:

"Oh! You should have seen us together on this moun-tain. We were so happy."

"But I did see you," I said.

"No, you didn't," she answered fiercely. "You only saw us when there were other people about, and that spoilt both it and us. Oh, I could talk to you for a year of the lovely things we did alone up here, in quiet secluded places

on this mountain." She paused. "We never wanted anyone else except Penelope."

She looked up at Penelope's basket still on the table. It
was the first time she had mentioned Penelope, and my
heart leapt at the sign. She paused again then, and said in
that remote voice: "You know what women say about
childbirth? Well, I just don't understand it. I have never
known such delight as having Penelope. There was not a
moment, not a second of her birth that was not sheer utter
joy to me. I just wanted to go on and on having more
children for Dicky. We were so *whole* together. Oh, God,
how can I ever become reconciled again to being only a
half for the rest of my life?"

I wished that I had had with me then some of the giant
intellects, some of the great addicts of pure reason. This
age, which is uniquely of their creation, has an answer for
everything. But I must confess that I had no answer
acceptable to the intellect. I had only a blind faith in
Val's, as in all our tears. I had only a blind faith in our
keeping together, closely, like sheep on the bitterest night
of winter, and humbly committing our helpless knowing
to the deep mystery of life.

At three o'clock in the morning our throats were so dry
from talking and general strain, that words would hardly
form themselves. Val was so exhausted that I believe if we
had had just one aspirin to give her she would have fallen
asleep. But she had none. It was so characteristic of her
and Vance and their absolute trust in the mountain that
they had no medicine of any kind in the hut; not even an
aspirin for themselves or dill-water for Penelope. My own
medicine, of course, was dumped with all the baggage in
the bottom of the Great Ruo gorge. Long afterwards
Quillan, talking about our vain search through the hut for
medicine, said to me:

"Even I would not trust Africa and Mlanje that far."

After one of these searches for medicine I went out, for a
moment, to the night. Above us the stars were bright, par-

ticularly Orion, Vance's "Old Hunter", high above Chambe Peak, prancing, with uplifted club, after the swift game of heaven. But away to the west, over the gorge, there were no stars, only that wheeling, twisting, turning, diabolic world of cloud. It was one of those suspended moments of reality when the universal pendulum is slowed down and the seconds, it seems, will not pass. I would have, had it seemed any good, reversed the last plea of the damned Faust and called on the horses of the night to hasten, to hasten, and bring up a rose-fingered dawn.

When I went back Val was still dreadfully becalmed and awake in her agony.

At half-past four Quillan went down to the foresters' huts, to fetch me a guide. We had agreed that he would stay with Val, get the natives to pack up her belongings and my tent, while I went to fetch help. Val was now so tired that she did not even hear my good-bye.

I pushed back the dogs who tried to come with me, patted them on the head, shut the door and stepped outside. There was just a faint lighting of the sky behind Chambe's own peak.

It was bitterly cold. We stepped out briskly. Fortunately my physical body had not needed sleep to be rested. We crossed the stream, treading Orion and the Milky Way underfoot, and quickly passed the cedars which, in their ancient resentment and deep disdain of men and their mission, stood still without even a rustle or a whisper.

We went as fast as we could down Vance's road, over his bridge, over the far edge and down the track. Dawn broke to reveal that same schism between light and dusk, fair and foul, over Mlanje. Half-way down we heard the first yodel and soon met the bearers coming up for their daily load.

At eight we knocked at the door of the house of Mrs. Carmichael, a friend of the Vances, who had a small tea-estate next to the forestry depot at Likabula. Down there the sun was already shining on her garden, and I shall never forget the scarlet of the poinsettias as the early light caught them. At the end of their long golden stems they burst on the blue and gold of the still morning air like pistol shots, disintegrations rather than fulfilments of the brightest red.

A native in a spotless white coat, so white that it hurt my tired eyes, came to the door, showed me into a room full of books, and said Mrs. Carmichael was coming at once.

Suddenly, as I sat there, through the open doors and windows a succession of cats of all sizes and shapes and colours came bounding into the room. I sat up with a shock. At first I thought I had fallen asleep and was dreaming, but as I counted thirty-one of them, and they all began begging for my attention, whining, miaowing, curving their spines, rubbing their shanks against my feet, jumping on my chair and waving their tails under my nose, I realized that I must be awake.

What my tired eyes were seeing was no disorder of my outraged senses, no midnight fantasy, but early morning on a tea-estate at the foot of Mlanje. And it seemed a needless, a derisory addition to the heavy adjustments my sense of reality had already to make. I had been on the go for thirty hours. In that time I had gone down the mountain, into that gorge, up it again, then done twenty miles over the top, and now twenty miles down it again, and all without sleep. Suddenly I resented the cats. It was all I could do to prevent myself from jumping up and putting my boot to them.

In desperation I looked over the arched backs and waving tails at some of the books. The first shelf began with all the volumes of Havelock Ellis' *Psychology of Sex*, and finished up with a book on sex symbolism by Krafft-Ebing.

My heart sank again. I said to myself: "Dear God! Everything you wish but not that! Please to-day send me people who are normal. Solid young men in tweeds and handlebar moustaches who, should they suddenly find themselves in Kubla Khan's harem, would read their *Times* first and finish their pipes before they so much as raised an eye to one coy beauty!"

Happily, at that moment Mrs. Carmichael came in. She had obviously just got up and was still in a dark blue dressing-gown. I was reassured at once by her appearance. The cats stopped miaowing the moment she appeared. I told her at once what had happened.

"Oh God. I was always afraid of it," she said, deeply moved. "I knew it would happen. I knew it. They just had something like it in them."

Her remarks helped me immensely. I could not, then, see why, but, in the days that followed, her remark often returned to me.

In five minutes she had dressed and we were in her big American car. I stopped at the depot just long enough to send some foresters with a stretcher up the mountain to fetch Val Vance. Then we drove at a great speed to the boma at Mlanje. Within a mile of Likabula we passed once more through the wall of the Chiperone and from there on were back in the rain and the whirling mist.

Boyd had left Mlanje but his successor got on to the telephone at once. The doctor was sent up to meet Val Vance. While I shaved, the police were organized. Those small European communities in Africa in moments of disaster close their ranks at once without forethought or hesitation. Everyone stopped work.

By nine I was going up the mountain through the mouth of the Great Ruo gorge with a large search-party. At eleven o'clock we were on the bank of the stream Vance had vainly tried to cross twenty-four hours before. There was our discarded baggage, black with rain, on the opposite bank, the rope of creepers that I had made Vance discard and the burnt-out ashes of Quillan's fire.

It was astonishing what a difference it made to one's reaction standing on the other bank, with a safe line of retreat at one's back. For a brief moment the sky lightened while we stood there. The place assumed the false, concentrated and exaggerated innocence of the truly wicked. But when I raised my eyes to the dark slopes behind and to the hidden peaks, and listened to the storm of noise raised by the falling water, I knew the mountain was unchanged and indifferent. It was as if the whole of Mlanje had been dematerialized and transformed into a kind of Tartar music, riding high, wide and diabolically handsome across the darkened steppes of heaven.

I turned my back on it for the last time without regret and joined in the search for Vance's body. As I and Quillan had expected, we found nothing. After a long, hopeless search, I went back to Blantyre and was with Argyle and Alan late that night.

I spent the Sunday helping Peter Quillan to organize Val Vance's affairs and booked her an immediate passage by air to England. It was not difficult because everybody wanted to help. Val was staying with the Quillans. Mary Quillan told me that the first night the doctor had had to give her three injections before she could sleep. She was a gallant girl.

When I went to say good-bye to Val and told her that we had not found Dicky's body, she said instantly: "I am so glad. I would prefer to think of him always there. He belonged to it."

"And you, Val, when you get home what are you going to do?" I asked her.

She didn't answer at once. She looked at Penelope on her lap, touched her cheek very lightly and then, staring out of the window into the rain and mist outside, said in a far-away voice: "Stay there for a bit and then come back to the mountain."

I knew then that she had turned her dangerous corner.

On the Monday I spent the whole morning doing Val's correspondence for her. It was my only chance because I had to resume my own journey at dawn on Tuesday.

In the afternoon and evening I sat by the fire in Alan's study writing a long technical report on my expedition to Mlanje. The fire was a fire of Blantyre wood and it burned in a lugubrious way so unlike the eager, gay, to-hell-with-you flame of the cedars.

I recommended in my report that Mlanje should be left to itself, to its mists, to its split weather, and to its cedars. I knew that, even had they known of my recommendation, those dark, resentful, desperate trees fighting for their antique being would not have thanked me. But I knew that Vance would have done.

PART IV

# BEYOND THE MOUNTAIN

"It seems to me that people's private and personal
lives have never mattered as they do now. For me
the whole of the future depends on the way people
live their personal rather than their collective lives.
It is a matter of extreme urgency. When we have
all lived out our private and personal problems we
can consider the next, the collective step. Then it
will be easy but before it will not even be possible."

LETTER FROM INGARET GIFFARD

# NYIKA PLATEAU

Karonga

Author's Route ➡

LAKE
NYASA

Chisiombe Bay

Ovenduwa R.
Jufira R.
Kasyowoyo R.
Weni Mweny
PLATEAU
6000

Mwesia R.
Chisali R.
Remero River

North Rukuru R.
Nundia R.
Kawawa River

5000-6000
MPANDA PEAK 7697

Njalowe
Njalowe

North
Njalowe
SAKOZYA PASS 7352

Ntawa R.
Wovwe or Fuliwa R.

Deep B.

CHITETE H.
Mpasi R.
IKAMPYONGO R. 6167
CHEKANGOMBE H. 5849
MHONA H. 5827
Jelindani

GRASS STEPPE
Domsawe Stm.
7826
Nkanta V.
8237

NGANDA H. 8697
KASANGA PK.

Mwatengara

Nhalanga V.
Fuliwa
MGOMBI H.

10°30'

Meetse R.
NORTHERN RHODESIA
KUWIKU H. 5815

Dohwe Plat.
Rukuru R. Channel
Chisango
Dambo
KHOWA H. 8228

Nkalanga

MASASSI H.
ARANGA H. 6597
KONGULA 7250
KANSAMPADDE PEAK 7106

Kaulime Pond
GRASS STEPPE
7916

MT LAWS

Livingstonia
Lion Point
Florence Bay

MT WALLER 4613
NARUH 4477

Chiveta

Ruwmba River
chira R.

NTAKATI H. 8257
LINTEKA H. 7071
CEJARAH 7190
KABARANGWE H. 8428

R. Rumi

R. Rumbi

KOMORI H.

MWANDA H. 7123
MAIN RD. TO FORT HILL
Katumbi

6960
Jaji R.

7000 TO 8000 FEET
Machimbula

Nchena-Chena

BANGWA H. 6484

BWANGOMBE

FINGIRA 8000
South Rukuru R.

USINWACA H. 6467
Mkondowi

BUMAO
6000
7356
KONJERO

Runyina R.

NGUNIKIRA H.
Owery R.

11° S.

34°0'
Njakwa

---

## Chapter Sixteen

IN order to get to the scene of my next task I now had to travel almost six hundred miles north, from one end of Nyasaland to the other. I had intended to go by road, but found on coming down from Mlanje that the people responsible for my travelling arrangements had taken a seat for me in an aircraft chartered to fly two extremely distinguished senior soldiers to the North. I was up and ready to leave at dawn on the Tuesday morning as arranged, but, as I listened to the rain and watched the mists swirl round Alan's sweet-peas, I knew we should not get away that day.

The weather that had contributed with such unnecessary and diabolic generosity to Vance's death was steadily thickening, and spreading from Mlanje far into the surrounding countryside. I was told on my return that the clouds did not disperse for thirty-five days. If, while waiting for the Chiperone to clear on Thursday, we had made the fire in the Ruo gorge as Vance's gunbearer had advised, or if we had made it on Friday as our own carriers had wanted, then, obviously, we should all have died.

The plane did not go on the Tuesday, the Wednesday or the Thursday, and, by the time I had unpacked and repacked again on Thursday night, I was a complete joke to the whole household. Yet, however anxious I was to go, my tired body was glad of the rest, and my mind was grateful for the chance to have Vance's death out with myself.

I found that I returned continually for comfort to two things: Mrs. Carmichael's remark, "It was in them"; and what Val had told me about Vance's childhood when we talked the reluctant seconds out that night by the fire. I do not want to harp on all this unnecessarily, but it was important to me and I cannot just pass it by.

From the moment Vance was killed I had blamed myself bitterly, though not for the actual accident. I think it is clear that there is a point at which all outside responsibility for an individual ends and the final event concerns him and his fate alone. Vance was twenty-eight, a soldier mentioned in dispatches in Burma, and an expert on the mountain. I do not believe that we were doing anything irresponsible in letting him attempt to cross the stream. From the moment he entered the water the game was between him and the mountain he loved.

It was rather in our being there at all, that I felt my share of the responsibility lay. Firstly, if I had not come out to Africa, Vance at that moment would in all probability not have been on the mountain. Secondly, if I had refused to let our party take the short-cut from the lumber camp, we should not have been in the gorge either. Then again I had had all the time an uneasy feeling about this trip. I had left England in a mood of resentment and had always been in a divided state about Africa. Supposing my own conflict about it had been resolved, could I have ever got entangled in a set of circumstances so disastrous as those on Mlanje?

My instinct was to say no; that a split in ourselves produces a split in the pattern of our lives, creates this terrible gash down the middle, this deep, dark Mlanje gorge, through which disaster runs and the devil drives. Accident and disaster without feed on accident and disaster within. The design of our outward life, from its minutest detail up to the atom which we put in our latest bomb, reflects and confirms our deepest and most private purposes.

I will give only one example. The world to my mind has never been fuller of finer thinking than it is to-day. I never pick up a paper, magazine or book, be they in Japanese,

French, Javanese, Russian, English or Twi, and fail to be struck by the fine thoughts, the idealistic feelings, the noble sentiments they express. Yet, though all the contributing writers appear to be merchants of man's finest feelings, has there ever been an age that, considering its lights, has done worse things than this one, with its class hatreds, race hatreds, colour prejudices, world wars and concentration camps? Has there been another age that, knowing so clearly the right things to do, has so consistently done the wrong ones?

I doubt it; and because I doubt it, I feel it is important as never before to get our private contribution to the split clear in our minds and, as far as possible, to close the gap in ourselves in every detail of our lives.

There was another curious point on the mountain. I had been afraid, and it had been for Val Vance that I feared and for her that I had taken precautions. But all my vigilance had been needed for ourselves; it was at our side, not hers, that disaster was creeping up. That too seemed typical of our age and its inheritors. Was it not the private equivalent of our public passion for effecting in others the cure we so badly need ourselves? Industrial England had once had a passion for converting the Africans of Nyasaland to Christian ways, which passion had increased in almost mathematical proportion to the un-Christian state of slavery in its own factories.

I could not help feeling that if I had been an utterly whole person that day in the gorge could never have existed.

Again when Mrs. Carmichael said, "I knew in my bones this would happen. They had it in them", she had shed a new light on the inner situation, as Val had done when she told me of her husband's past. Now I saw the real significance of Val's remarks about Vance's childhood. He had never been happy or even spasmodically at one with his home. He had always felt that he was rather looked down upon. This was no grown-up fantasy on Val's part. She had known Vance as a child, and could remember that even then people had never really understood him, or appreciated his qualities. It had always infuriated her to see him so underrated and held back by the opinion of quite inferior men.

After the war he had returned to marry her, as he had always wanted, and at once brought her to Mlanje. There for the first time he seemed to blossom out, and to be living in a free way of his own making. That is why they were so happy there, and, she hinted, why they liked to be alone. The presence of outside people, however pleasant, tended to revive in their lives the pattern of a past they had hoped to be done with for good, brought back responses and reactions of a discredited inferiority no longer their own. For she too had not had the happiest of lives until their marriage.

It had been perfect for them on the mountain. There, and in themselves, they found everything they had ever wanted; and in this perfection they meant to live till the end. She almost gave me the impression that they were refugees from their own past, thinking they could rid themselves of the problem of their lives by changing their location; believing they only had to go far enough away and they would leave their problem behind them. How little those unfortunate children of life knew of the hound of unfulfilled nature within the blood that is for ever on our trail, ready to aid and abet the dark fates without.

Now I shall never know any more detail about the life of that brave, upright young man; but it seems to me certain from what I know already, that sooner or later there was bound to be a reckoning between himself and his nature which I could not influence, save as an instrument of the inevitable. On Friday at ten-thirty in the Great Ruo gorge of Mlanje the unpredictable in himself and the unpredictable in the mountain, the split in himself and the dark gash in Mlanje met and became one.

When I reached this point I felt better. I do not pre-

tend that this is a final solution. I am sure that to a heart
and an awareness less clouded than my own there must be
much more to understand. But I myself could take it no
further. After all, one can never take anything far enough.
If one is lucky one takes things as far as one can. This I
had done, and a limited reassurance was mine. I needed
it too; indeed I shall always need it. That moment in the
gorge has become a part of me. I shall have to live with
it to the end of my life. Nor is it the only moment of its
kind. There have been quite a number of other moments
equally grim. Of these I need say no more now, except
perhaps that they have a habit of all massing together
and presenting themselves to my senses at the most unexpected moments; waking me up at midnight, making
me hesitate in my steps across a crowded street, or perhaps just making me stroke the head of a neighbour's dog
with unusual tenderness.

When they do that it is necessary to relive them again in
some way, to look them squarely in their eyes, to take them
by the hand in an avowal of a sad friendship, and say
"How are you now? Better? Is there anything more I
can do for you?" and at a shake of a dark head, to reply
encouragingly before continuing on one's way, "Perhaps
it will be better next time. Perhaps it will pass." This does
not sound much. But it is all one can do, and it helps even
if it does not cure.

At least having got so far in my mind I was able to sleep.
I had my first good night for some time.

I woke to see the rain still coming down. At half-past
nine I was suddenly summoned to the aerodrome. It
appeared that twelve miles out the sky was lightening,
though round me there was no sign of it.

I got to Chileka to find the pilot in consultation with
the meteorological officers on the aerodrome. Archie
Gordon, a young South African from Grahamstown, was
very much worried. He was already three days overdue.
He was getting angry messages from his superiors in

Salisbury. They were, this private charter firm, a new pioneer organization struggling for a living and could not afford to annoy their clients. In addition, the two distinguished soldiers had become awkward and were also urging him not to delay another instant.

The pilot obviously did not like the idea. He told me he had already had a nasty experience coming through from Rhodesia on the Monday. He had then taken a grave risk for the sake of "the firm", as he loyally called it, but had not minded it as he had been alone.

As he approached Blantyre he had seen this extraordinary pillar, this dark turning, revolving, spinning pillar of cloud over Mlanje and the surrounding country. At seventeen thousand feet in his little single-screw plane he had given up trying to get above it. He had no ground control at Chileka to help him down. He had just trusted to his luck and his reckoning and put the plane's nose down into the cloud. He said it was as black as night and as turbulent as hell inside, but his luck held and he came down slap bang on the aerodrome. But it was not a risk he would ever like to take again.

As I listened to all this I had an uncanny feeling that once again I was in a workshop of Fate, so that when he turned to me and asked appealingly in my native Afrikaans what I thought of it, I said clearly: "Look, you must on no account take what seems too great a risk to you. If you think as a technician that the risk is too great, I would let no power on earth make you change your mind."

"But aren't you all in a hurry?" he said—relieved, I thought.

"I am not in a hurry to kill or be killed," I replied. "Whether you think we should not go or should go, I will trust you implicitly. I will back up any decision you take, to the full."

He seemed enormously cheered by this and said he would just go up for five minutes and see what it felt like "on top".

While he was up, the two generals telephoned from Blantyre. They were at the hotel. Was there or was there not to be a flight? If not, why not?

The duty officer replied that it was still uncertain. Very well then, they would wait at the hotel and wanted the pilot to telephone them, as soon as he came down.

"I don't like it at all," said Gordon when he did so. "It is all right for the moment here but it is piling up, and bearing down fast, all round the place."

He spoke on the telephone, put the receiver down, with a very sour South African schoolboy face, that made me warm to him, and said: "Those two old Donners[1] don't like it. They want to go, and want to see me at once."

"Never mind," I told him. "You do what you think is right, and all will be well. Besides, the war is over and no one will thank you for killing two such distinguished soldiers, though they might be prepared to overlook the death of a half-colonel."

It was still raining in Blantyre. The two generals were sitting by the fire in the hotel lounge. They did not look pleased. One was General Brere-Adams, whom I knew from the Far East and for whom I have the greatest admiration and affection; the other, General Braidie, whom I hardly knew. Waiting, however, had got on their nerves and neither was at his best.

When the pilot told them politely and with great—I thought, almost exaggerated—deference that he did not think it was wise to take off, General Braidie, the General I did not know, stood up, thrust his hands deep in his pockets, tapped the ground with his right foot, looked straight past the pilot with a shiny eye, and said: "Oh! Yes. So I have been told too: the whisky in Blantyre is better than in Salisbury, and there's plenty of it!"

General Brere-Adams, the one I knew, softened his

---

[1] Donner, literally thunder, is the Afrikaans equivalent of the Australian "Bastard". It can be either a term of great affection or extreme abuse. On this occasion, I do not think it was a term of affection.

remark with a smile and a sly upward glance from essentially friendly eyes, but it was to the same point: "Is she
so very nice? Is she dark or fair?"

I was getting increasingly angry at all this and said
firmly that I thought they were being extremely unfair to
the pilot. It wasn't easy for him to say "no" to two such
distinguished people, whom he obviously wanted to please,
and what he needed was not their arm-chair judgment but
understanding. Besides, I had been out at the aerodrome,
spoken to the weather officers myself, and there was no
doubt that flying anywhere would be a risky business. I
spoke with some warmth and annoyed General Braidie,
who snorted at every sentence I spoke, and was very rude
to me afterwards. But we did not fly.

At lunch I told the two generals not to count on my
sharing their charter any more. I was going to make
arrangements to go north at once by road. I did not tell
them so, but I had seen enough that day of the sort of considerations, the flippant, irrelevant considerations, which
could determine flights of the kind we had been trying to
make. Africa jerks the European out of his own true centre
and makes him accident-prone. I was glad to be out of it.

To my surprise General Braidie too said he had had
enough of the aircraft and could he join in with me by
road? Between us we managed to arrange for a car to take
us north the following morning, and for the first time I felt
completely free of the cycle of events which started a week
before with that unfortunate short-cut over the Ruo
valley of Mlanje.

## Chapter Seventeen

THE main road north from Blantyre to Fort Hill and Tanganyika is long, broad and normally dusty, but there was little dust on the southern end of it that Saturday morning as we piled all our gear into a station wagon and set out on our journey. Our party consisted of General Braidie, a foreman-joiner for a vast development prospect up north, a bricklayer foreman, and myself.

The car was grossly overloaded and danced like a frightened horse from one end of the slippery road to the other. The black driver called himself Lincoln, and was at once christened Abraham by the bricklayer foreman, who was fresh from the army of occupation in Germany. This driver quickly lost his nerve and asked in rather plaintive Swahili if I wouldn't like to take over. So I did.

Luckily about fifty miles from Blantyre we passed out of the mist and the rain, and we could see the cloud standing like a wall over the land away to our right. The station wagon, however, continued to be tricky on the steering and I had no time for sight-seeing. Yet the general impression of the country seen through the windscreen or from snap glances to right and left was very beautiful.

Africa communicates its own enormous sense of relief to one when it shakes itself free from towns, and the ease with which it now unfolded its great vistas of bush, valley, hills and plains was most exhilarating. I felt like singing and even General Braidie seemed inclined to step out of his specialized view of himself and others.

At half-past twelve we were climbing out of the great Shire valley, the deep depression along which Lake Nyasa empties its surplus water. We went through Ncheo, on the flank of the long, blue, elegant Kirk ranges, just at one o'clock. It was market day and the bazaars were full of natives dressed up in their brightest colours. There is no skin in the world for showing up colours like a really black one, and these people of the foothills are not only born black but burnt blacker still by the intolerable and fanatic sun of the Nyasaland summers.

Seldom, I thought, had I seen red so red, yellow so yellow and green so green, as in these cloths which the natives of Ncheo wrapped around themselves like Roman togas.

The women walked demurely behind their men, with that trance-like motion produced in them by the necessity for balancing the heavy earthen jars on their heads. They were vivid, eager creatures. The sly passing glances they gave us out of the corners of their eyes were gay and bright with awareness of their sex.

"Gosh, sir," I heard the foreman-joiner say to General Braidie: "it is a good thing the sun is not out, or those colours would strike you blind."

Outside Ncheo we climbed up on to one of the higher spurs of the Kirk range, pulled up by a large spreading acacia and had some lunch.

It was very beautiful. We saw the southern end of Lake Nyasa looking like the sea with a beginning but no end to it. We saw the whole of Lake Malombe and the vast Shire depression, lapped by a deep tide of winter-blue light. It was an orchestration of blues, almost of Whistler Battersea blues, and looked empty of human beings and terribly indifferent to them.

The road then took us on to the wide, towering plains of the Angoni highlands. Here spirals of spinning dust impelled by a cold south-west wind patrolled the roads and tracks. Again the background was an immense forlorn blue, the foreground lion-coloured. There were plenty of black figures in rags and tatters about, walking from nowhere to no obvious destinations. They looked so homeless that the view quickly resumed the forlorn, abandoned quality of the depression below Ncheo.

On these plains I always feel a private disappointment. The people who inhabit them are of Zulu origin, the descendants of one of the terrible Chaka's Impis. They mutinied and raided north on a venture of their own, plundering bare an immense track of Africa, from Zululand to the southern shore of Victoria Nyanza. They are utterly unlike our Zulus in the South to-day, having none of their robustness of body and spirit; they seem shrunken and cowed as if to them, too, this part of Africa had brought no joy, only deception.

Here were our first koppies too, the stragglers from those isolated hills of stone which are such a feature of the vast central plateau of Africa. They added their own touch of aloofness to the scene. And it got cold, very cold.

We passed round the foot of the broad flanks of the freakish outcrop of Mount Dedza, but dared not go into the village because it was getting late. Going as fast as the dancing station wagon would let us, we got to the hotel at the little provincial capital of Lilongwe just as the sun, pink with cold, went down behind a long line of green and white thorn trees.

At dawn on Sunday morning we swung back into the road to the North. There was a crisp, frosty dew sparkling on the bleached grass; and a halo of honey-gold hung round the acacia-tops. The scene did not change much. What was remarkable was this quality of "unendingness".

One would climb out on a rise, round a hill or cross a river, expecting it to have changed, for it had looked the same for hundreds of miles, but there it would be, repeating itself with the same blue, melancholy satisfaction.

We passed no cars and saw no European, except at one bridge, where we found a Greek planter sitting with a gun in his hand. He looked yellow with fever and rather desperately ill. There was, he told us, all around there, a lot of sleeping sickness.

We drove like this from dawn until four in the afternoon, and all the while my companions seemed to me to be changing somewhat. They seemed to be acknowledging instinctively the great pre-eminence, the absolute priority of the physical fact of Africa, and the relative unimportance of human beings in the scheme of things around us. They became very quiet, depressed and stared continuously with defensive eyes at a landscape that offered no easy assurances. In that mood, at four precisely, we drove into Mzimba, the capital of the northernmost province of Nyasaland.

We spent the night with Charles Drackersby, the District Commissioner in Mzimba. He was out when we arrived, but Jock Standing, the resident engineer of the great Tung Development scheme in the Vipya highlands at Msusi, where the General was going, met us and took us straight to the D.C.'s home. I now gathered from him that we were none of us going to be very welcome at Msusi. John Grantham, his manager, had said firmly when he heard of our coming that he would tolerate no more impositions from London.

It all sounded very depressing there in Mzimba on that blue Sunday afternoon. If John Grantham really wouldn't help, it would be serious for me. I should have to retrace my steps all those hundreds of miles to Blantyre, plan again and start out anew. There was obviously nothing I could do as an alternative in Mzimba. The so-called towns on the map, strung out like beads on a red and black necklace, were not only getting farther apart, but desperately small.

Mzimba, in fact, was not a bead so much as a small seed, a mustard seed of administrative faith, on a thin and rapidly diminishing string of civilization. It consisted of no more than a dozen European bungalows, hurriedly built of unburned brick; a few Indian stores, an old boma waving a defiant bright new Union Jack at the black bush around; an old commissioner's house with a few impudent poinsettias and purple bougainvilleas to distinguish it, themselves only a slight variation in the prevailing winter-blue theme of the atmosphere. For the rest it was idle to ignore that Africa was reasserting itself with increasing confidence, with a certain air of dark, sullen triumph.

Meanwhile I wondered what Drackersby could do to help. He got back at five: apparently he spent all the time he could in the bush. He was burnt black by years of service under the Nyasaland sun and had a wiry, out-of-doors look. Before he came over to us, he slowly opened the boot of his car, pulled out a small dead buck, and threw it down on the veranda of his bungalow. Apart from a polite greeting, he hardly spoke to us until he had cleaned his guns. That done, nobody could have been pleasanter or more interesting.

As far as I was concerned, however, Drackersby said nothing to encourage me. He had the same complaint about the lack of understanding in the capital, the same grievance that people like Grantham and himself were having too much asked of them. He didn't know what the hell London was about, sending me out in the winter. Didn't they realize it was cold in Africa?

"You won't get any natives to go up the Nyika with you," he said. "If you do, you will probably kill them, and yourself."

I winced inwardly at that. I myself had told him of the tragedy at Mlanje. I don't think he knew how deeply he had hurt me. For a moment the whole of that tragic Friday came back to me, and I could only say quietly: "Surely the cold is only relative. I always prefer the cold in Africa to the mud."

I honestly believe he had never thought of that, and was taken aback. He gaped at me with some surprise for a moment and then snapped: "Anyway, relative or not, you won't get any Africans to go with you."

He must have thought differently of it in the night,

however, for he gave me the next morning a letter to the Chief Katumbi, whose people live near the foot of the great Nyika Plateau. The letter was very much to the point, and asked the chief plainly, in the name of the government, to help me.

"He will get you bearers if anybody can," he said. "But do not bank on it."

I left Mzimba at ten o'clock and drove straight into another cold, overcast day of expanding blue. About twenty miles out the bush fell away from us and the road began to twist among grey, elegant hill-tops, covered only with grass. The relief to the eyes was immense. For nearly a hundred miles the jeep, purring like a kitten, took us through highlands which had something of Scotland about them, but they were unmistakably African in their dark valleys dense with black, lichen-festooned, shrunken trees.

After driving fifty miles I saw one red brick house and farm buildings, obviously European. I thought their little settlement looked dreadfully hemmed in, pinned down by Africa, and I wondered how it would ever stand up to that sort of siege.

On the way I passed the cattle: I noticed they were grazed in a tight formation with three sturdy black men armed with long, broad spears, standing guard over them. They and their masters were the first living things I had seen for fifty miles, an island of threatened animal life in a sea of grass, trees, stone and grey hill-tops.

I travelled almost another fifty miles before I saw another living soul or human habitation of any kind. If it had not been for some lonely buzzard slowly circling the grey sky with geometric precision, I should have thought the land empty of animals too.

When I drove up at four, John Grantham, the General and Jock Standing were talking in a group outside Grantham's house at Msusi. But for the black, lichen-strewn jungle all around, I could easily have taken the patch of clearing that was Msusi to be somewhere in England. Grantham's little house and the four other houses around were all built of near-red brick, with tall, sloping thatched roofs. There were rambler-roses growing up the porch of Grantham's cottage, violets against the walls, a garden in front full of lupins, foxgloves, antirrhinums, sweet williams, London Pride and carnations. The grey mist which smokes over everything in winter there on the summit of the Vipya highlands added to the European effect.

Grantham himself could only have been a product of the British Isles. To my astonishment he immediately held out his hand and in a pleasant civilized voice said: "Come on in! I have kept some lunch for you. I believe you are someone whom I can really talk to about Africa, and not be misunderstood."

The next thirty-six hours were for me some of the most pleasant I had spent in Nyasaland. We discovered we had known each other many years before when, fresh from the 1914–18 air-force and Cambridge, he had come to plant cotton in Zululand. The last he had heard of me was a report that I had been killed in action against the Japanese.

In these twenty-four years John Grantham had done many things, but as he sat by the fire with Papillon, his black spaniel, on his knees, he said that, varied as they had been, and however different from what he had planned, their effect had all been the same—to take him deeper and deeper into Africa.

The cotton experiment had been a total failure, as I knew. After that he had tried his hand at farming in Southern Rhodesia. That had gone well until the girl he was going to marry, climbing a koppie on his farm one day, scratched her knee on a rock, contracted blood poisoning and died within ninety-six hours.

Nothing had gone right after that. He went ranching for some years in Northern Rhodesia. A succession of droughts finished that phase of his life. His capital was exhausted. The outlook was dismal.

Then the war came and, of course, like all the rest of us, he joined up, rose to the dizzy rank of regimental sergeant-major in a reconnaissance unit, and finally was blown up by a mine in his armoured car in North Africa, and forced to leave the Army. Then the Nyasaland Government claimed his services, and in due course he was sent to start this big Tung experiment in the heart of the misty, un-populated Vipya. It was a job after his own heart. He was alone, except for the black labour he could raise. The Africans knew him, liked him, trusted him, and came to him readily, far more of them than he could use. All the clearing of the bush, all that eighty miles of road over mountain-top, and through valley and jungle, was all his own work. He had enjoyed it, but now the place was getting too crowded. He already had three other Euro-peans, and more were coming. He couldn't stand that. Africa was where he wanted to live and die, if, he grumbled, it did not get too crowded.

And yet there was a tremendous paradox in this. And in so far as the facts of my journey imposed a theme on it from within, this paradox is most relevant to it. This is why I have sketched Grantham in detail here.

All the texture of his mind, the weave of his spirit, the very dream he was living on the Vipya, that high country, which smokes with mist as its native name implies, was essentially European.

Every detail of the room in which we sat testified to this. Over the fireplace were stuck picture postcards of Suffolk and its villages. There was also an old ticket to the mem-bers' enclosure at Newmarket, and a torn-off London theatre ticket. The guns, bright and clean in the rack; the fishing rods with their many flies, and dozens of others from the British Isles, all delicately and temperately coloured; the port; the sherry decanter filled with Bristol Cream; the barometer; the spy-glass; the books and the smell of dogs, were all part and parcel of a European approach to life.

The point of it all, so it seemed to me, was this. People like Grantham could no longer sustain Europe; they needed, in a manner which is not yet clear to me, the support of Africa; the presence of black faces and black natures confirms their vision, their old, essentially European dream. It was as if, by losing themselves in Africa, they re-established the solidity and significance of the European in themselves.

As far as detailed help for my own journey was concerned, I found Grantham had lived for five years at the foot of the Nyika, the plateau which I had to look over. He had never been on it—"a hell of an expedition" he said. But he knew all the native gossip about it. They were terrified of it. It was high, it was misty, it had tremendous encounters with rain and thunder. It was cold, and was said to be completely uninhabited and rather sinister.

If one listened to the natives talking about Nyika one always heard about some tragedy connected with it. They would say, for example: "You know old Bathikutha? Well, he is no more. He tried to go over the Nyika three days after the last moon. The clouds came down and he has not been seen since."

They also believed there was a large snake living in a small lake on top of it. If one could touch its tail when one was ill, this cured one instantly, but if one went there for no good reason, the snake caught and carried one off to its hole in the bottom of the lake.

Yet they did sometimes go to hunt on the fringes of the plateau by day. They said it was full of game. He thought he could get me bearers from Katumbi's people. He would give me a letter too, for Katumbi. What was more, he would present me with his own personal jeep, Peaches, his own native driver, and his own hunting boy, Patrick, one of the Katumbi's own people who would recruit bearers for me. His stores, he said, were nearly empty since the lake steamer which brought them to Nkata Bay, about seventy miles away, was grossly overdue. But I was most welcome to what he had. He only wished he could come himself, but with such a crowd about he had no time. I did understand that, didn't I? And now, when was I last in Zululand?

# Chapter Eighteen

I LEFT Msusi by jeep in a thick, blue mist thirty-six hours after my arrival on the Tuesday morning. We all sat in front. Once back on the road to Fort Hill we went really fast. We passed through several small native settlements, and everywhere the population came to attention, as it were, when we went by; bowed if they were old, raised their hats if they had any, and then brought them down to hang respectfully in their hands by their sides.

A hard, cold wind tore down the road outside Enk-wendeni. We went straight into it at forty-eight miles an hour, and left a high column of dust rising in the air be-hind us. We were off the highlands now, had done with physical eccentricities like the Vipya, and once again there began the prevailing African theme of bush, plain, river and lone blue hill, until suddenly, about sixty miles away, I saw the Nyika.

Everything at that distance looks small, and yet I found my pulse quickening at the view. There was a sort of Rider Haggard, a King Solomon's Mines, a Queen of Sheba touch about it. A massive, long, blue escarpment, a wall of solid, unbroken mountain rose sheer out of the land and lost itself in the clouds. This wall became bigger, more precise, but did not change. Still its cloud-capped blue towered unbroken in the forefront of our vision. Only at Njakwa—another native township nearly seventy miles further on—we were nearly at the base of it, at last.

Hard by Njakwa, we crossed the rumbling Rumpi. This was my first encounter with a river that rose some-where in the clouds above, on the Nyika. It cut a deep gash through the fifteen-hundred-foot hills around Njakwa, and we drove straight up along the northern flank of it, and on towards Katumbi. Here we were too close to the hills to see the great wall of the Nyika, but our senses were perfectly aware of it in the background. Our eyes knew it from the colour and texture of that dense concentration of cloud to the north, our noses from a certain tingling in the nostrils, our ears from a singing in the drums, a sound almost like the purring of a large purple cat near at hand, and our bodies from a mounting excitement in the blood. So abstracted were we that at midday we nearly ran over a long, elegant, naked black body stretched out in the middle of the road.

I saw it first, and shouted to Peaches to stop. He managed to do this just at the body's feet. It did not move. We all three looked down in amazement over the top of the windscreen, on a lovely young, black, female body, stark naked, in the road. At first I feared it was dead, but then noticed it was breathing deeply and was asleep. Peaches, who was roaring like a lion, leapt out of the jeep and shook it angrily. Slowly it sat up and rubbed its eyes, and then out of them looked a young woman who, quite undismayed, began making advances to Peaches. Patrick and he had to carry her off the road, where she continued to invite us to join her with looks, smiles, wriggles and other gestures. I have never seen anyone of her sex so completely and so happily drunk at that hour of the day.

Patrick explained that the harvest was on, and people always drank like that at harvest-time. He shook his head. It might be difficult to get bearers after all.

As we drove into the native town of Katumbi and stopped outside the Chief's court-house, the entire population seemed to drop what they were doing in order to pour out of their huts and run towards us. Their curiosity was quite unashamed but most friendly. They did not see a white face every day and were determined to make the most of mine. They pressed round the jeep and commented on my physical appearance: "Did you ever see such coloured hair?" "How big his nose is!" "Look at his eyes. His cheeks are very red! Is he angry, you think?" "How much do you think that coat of his cost?" and so on endlessly.

Meanwhile I sent Patrick to see if the chief, the Um-fumo, was there. He came back with one Patrick Ka-wonga, the clerk of the Umfumo's court, a handsome young man, pleasant, polite, but again with such a melancholy expression on his face that I knew he must be very well educated. I was not mistaken. He told me in clear, precise English that the Umfumo was away but that he would deal with the situation as best he could. I thanked him and decided there and then not to return to Msusi or Nzimba but to go straight on to Karonga, the northernmost province of Nyasaland, leaving Patrick behind me. I had come prepared to do that if necessary. I also had with me a letter to the D.C. there, and Alan had asked me to call on his Veterinary Officer at Karonga, a Michael Dowler, who would help me.

I took out my map and studied it carefully. This was not difficult. Facts, reliable facts, on maps of this part of Africa are few and far between. Karonga was too far for that day, but my eye fixed on Nchena-Chena, the agricultural research station at the foot of the Nyika, about thirty miles from the Rumpi gorge. The officer in charge of it, Colonel Henderson, was an old friend of Grantham's. If he was away, I would either sleep on the road or try and cadge a night's lodging at Livingstonia, another twenty or thirty miles further on, and the greatest of Nyasaland's mission stations.

At a quarter-past five the jeep drew up outside Colonel Henderson's house, Nyasaland Office-of-Works emergency pattern. The evening was closing in rapidly. Behind the house, almost from the kitchen doorstep, the land gathered itself together steeply, and rose covered with forest like a dark, blue-green wall seven thousand feet high, sheer into the cloud. All round about was the sound

of falling, running water, and now more strongly than ever
I had a sense that behind the wall of mountain and beyond the cloud, a gigantic purple cat was purring and
purring with an incurable smugness and satisfaction.

I could not on this first close contact with the Nyika
understand why it should be thought sinister. Mlanje had
given me the creeps from the start by its quality of ill-
suppressed prehistoric rage. The feeling here was different, not friendly, just utterly self-contained and satisfied.

Wherever I had met Henderson I should have known
him for what he was, a soldier formed in the 1914–18 war.
When, as a mere boy in the late Edwardian world, he first
went to Sandhurst, it had been his ambition to make a
career of soldiering. The war cured him of that. He had
joined the agricultural department of Nyasaland. He had
made two blades of grass grow where one grew before—
and I use that phrase deliberately because Swift's sentence
from which it is taken was nailed like a flag to the wall over
his desk.

Henderson, too, knew the Nyika. He had, years before,
laid down an experimental pyrethrum plot on the lip of
the plateau, just behind his house, eight thousand two
hundred feet up. The soil was fertile. He had grown crops
equal to the world's best, but in the end let the work lapse
because he could not get the Africans, for whom it was
done, to go there.

"I don't know what it is," he said, "but they will not
live on the Nyika at any price. It is, as far as we know,
completely uninhabited."

He was gloomy about my finding bearers to go with me.
The harvest was on. It was cold, the old story. He thought
I was wasting my time going to Karonga, the people of
those hot plains would go with me least of all.

I made up my camp bed in Henderson's office that
night, but before going to sleep, went outside to look at
the mountains at the back. I could not see them, but again
I felt their presence deep in the nerves of my body. I sat

there for quite a while on a stone, being aware of them, and listening to the sound of infinitely falling water. Then, for the first time since my arrival in Nyasaland, I heard African drums warming up. I could see no fires, but everywhere in the black bush around the drums began. The tap-a-tap, tap-a-tap-tap-tap would break out in one place and then be answered in dozens of others near and far. As the night went on the drumming gathered speed, density and power. The darkness vibrated with its urgency. The sound of it, the purring of the great purple cat behind the clouds and the beat of my own heart harmonized so well, that I was soon sound asleep.

The next day we started early. The road moved all along the base of the Nyika itself. On our left was that sheer wall of mountain, its head buried in cloud; on our right a deep depression cut by the Rumpi and Rukuru rivers, and on their far side again was another chain of massive mountains. It presented everywhere a solid, unyielding, unbroken front that was quite unbelievable. I could see no obvious way up—in fact it looked as if there could not be one. Yet my task was concerned with the unknown summit. I noticed that native cultivation did little more than touch the fringe of the base of the Nyika. It was too steep and too densely covered with rain-forest even for native hoes.

An hour later we began climbing a flat-topped hill of about four thousand feet, which suddenly barred our way to the east. We climbed down and out of two deep valleys cut into its sides by the Rumpi—another Rumpi—and the Mwanana Rumpi, and by a series of steep hairpin bends reached the top. There I made Peaches stop, and looked back.

We were high up now, and the Nyika looked twice the size it had looked from below. In order to appreciate the greatness of these mountains properly, one must oneself have achieved a certain height. Below there is no standard of comparison, but once one is some thousands of feet up

the vastness of their scale becomes apparent and takes
away one's breath.

For thirty miles, as far as I could see, there was nothing
but this unbroken wall of mountain, standing on the tip of
its toes on the edge of a great depression, its head in the
clouds.

Only opposite me, where the two new rivers emerged,
was there a tremendous split in the mountain wall which
went back as far as I could see, hemmed in from rain-
forest base to glistening grey cloud-tops.

Away to our right and on our own level, lay the great
mission station of Livingstonia. To our mountain-,
plain- and bush-fed eyes, its neat, red-tiled roof-tops and
great cathedral walls rising above the acacia and bracha-
stygea fringe of the horizon, it was an astonishing sight.
It looked a brave, if terribly small, European gesture, a
small clenched fist shaken at the world of giants around.

I had always wanted to visit it but felt I couldn't do so
until some of the "ifs" were removed from my task. So
regretfully I told Peaches to drive on.

Three miles further we came over the top and started
going down. Then the sun suddenly came out. We were
emerging from underneath the umbrella of cloud that lay
on the mountains. We rounded a corner and saw Lake
Nyasa. I have seen it many times from the air, from far-
off mountain-tops and remote passes in the hills, but I had
never been so near.

Three thousand sheer feet down there it was, that
miracle of so much water in the midst of so much land. Indeed Lake Nyasa is a sea rather than a lake, and when one
has said that, there is, as about the sea itself, nothing further
to add which is neither an anticlimax nor bathos. Only
on that morning it was a singularly gay sight. Very blue
and sparkling in the sun, and with the far blue summits of
the great Livingstone range, on the far eastern side about
fifty miles away, pressing like Alps around, there was about
it something of the Mediterranean in the spring. Away to

the south, as far as the eye could reach, there was just blue water and nothing else. High as we were, we could hear the waves pounding the shore, as if they were indeed sea-waves. We started down eagerly towards the lake.

The road dropped down the face of a three-thousand-foot cliff. It was cut into the mountain side in a series of desperate zigzags. There were twenty-three of these inclines, each half a mile long; and when we looked up from below, our descent and, still more, the construction of the road itself, seemed an almost impossible feat. Yet that road was not the product of modern engineering. It was a product of missionary faith and zeal, built many years ago by believing amateurs with the help only of unskilled, unbelieving Africans.

At the foot of the escarpment the road swung away sharply to the north. We travelled slowly because it was so broken. For sixty miles it followed close by the lake shore on our right, whilst on our left was the wall of the Nyika, its cap of grey cloud still pulled down firmly about its ears. But as the plain between water and mountain widened it seemed to swing away in giant strides to the north-east.

It got hot. At first the country was thickly populated and desperately over-cultivated, but afterwards for most of the way it was nothing but shimmering grey bush, pale with sunlight on its long white thorns, and only splashed with colour where it showed a baobab tree or two, like a birthmark on its sallow cheeks. It shimmered, trembled and danced incessantly in the heat, and it was deathly silent whenever the shrill cicada hymn to sun and thorn would allow it. At four in the afternoon, the Nyika well out of sight, we drove into the native town of Karonga.

An immense crowd of black people was surging over the landing strip in the centre of the town. Drums were beating, people singing, shouting battle cries and blowing shrill whistles. All over the place, independent bands and teams of natives, with baboon tails and leopard claws tied round their middles in all possible varieties of jungle fantasy, danced, leapt, swirled and stamped their feet, roaring deep down in their stomachs with a mad, ecstatic abandon. Neither Peaches nor I knew what to make of it.

We might have been alarmed, since the commotion and noise were terrific, but for the fact that nowhere was there a policeman or a uniform of any kind to be seen, and that the black people who were not actually dancing, leaping, shrieking, beating drums or ceaselessly blowing whistles, were dressed in the favourite flaming colours of their best clothes. Then suddenly I saw three topees, three European heads, floating like the corks of a fishing net on this heaving sea of twelve thousand black, prancing figures.

No one appeared to have noticed my arrival. I got out of the jeep and went among the crowd. The noise was deafening, but it was the sweetest-smelling, the cleanest African crowd I had ever been among. I suddenly felt how lovely it was to be among so many people and no longer sitting silently in a prancing jeep, holding myself back from a too great awareness of the aggressive, disturbing physical qualities of Africa. The feeling warmed me through like wine, gave me a feeling of being a sort of ancient mariner walking among a goodly company.

I slowly made my way to the three topees. When I got near, I saw that they were deeply concerned in a tug-of-war. Two of them, nice-looking, clean-shaven Englishmen, in spotlessly neat khaki shorts and shirts, were directing operations, whilst a third, with a long, lean, sensitive face, grey eyes and a small cavalry moustache, his hair perhaps just a shade too long, was sitting at ease rather nonchalantly on a shooting stick and just watching them. The glow, the smile, in his wide grey eyes, however, belied his nonchalant pose of his body. A very tall African of about six foot eight was helping the other two. He was wearing dark suede shoes with plum-coloured stockings, fine navy shorts, a yellow silk shirt and green silk muffler. He had a gold watch on his wrist and a Livingstone-Stanley topee in his hand.

The two teams were keen. They faced each other like Angoni Impis going to war. The crowd was wildly excited. Both sides pulled with such a will and the crowd roared such encouragement that thrice they pulled apart a rope the size of a ship's cable, and to everyone's huge delight the two teams landed in a heap in the dust. It was a wonderful laugh that followed. It rang out absolutely instantly and spontaneously, like a loud peal from a bell hung in that blue sky over us. I felt like beginning to dance myself.

Suddenly I heard the older of the two Englishmen say to the other, in an agonized voice: "For God's sake, Jerry, go and hide the prizes quickly! We shan't get a decision. We have no thicker rope."

"Can't we give them all prizes?" asked Jerry, hesitating.

The other scratched his chin and said, "It's rather a lot of money, you know. I'm not sure I can afford to spend any more. . . ."

"Don't let us worry about that," said Jerry, now dead keen, "I would like to come in fifty-fifty with you."

The man on the shooting stick seemed the least engaged, so I went over to him, introduced myself, and asked for Michael Dowler.

"I am Dowler," he said. "I am delighted. I have been expecting you. Come and meet the others. What do you think of our family?" he added, as we shook hands. "We have given the whole town a day off—King's birthday, of course."

# Chapter Nineteen

I SPENT the night with Michael Dowler, in his house on the edge of the landing-strip, now empty, black and silent. Because of the damp and the heat the house was built on two floors like the old-fashioned, lakeside houses, and was closed in from head to foot with mosquito wire netting.

The lake was close by. The moment we stopped speaking, the noise of the waves on the shore, a short, choppy, lapping noise, like the sea on an East Coast Channel beach, came in through the wide open doors and windows behind the mosquito netting, and spread throughout the house. The house itself smelt strongly of bats. Dowler carried on an intermittent war against them, but they were prolific and determined. Their smell, no matter what he did, penetrated everywhere: an acrid, ancient smell which touched, inside oneself, some fearful, obscure instinct beyond experience and knowing. Every now and then there would be a rush of their wings in the dark outside, followed by a burst of high-pitched squeaking, almost too sharp for human ears to bear. And all night long there was the sound of native drums: people drumming by the dark lake shore, drumming on the outskirts of the town and far back in the bush, which was now quite dark, with ranks closed tightly against the night and its arrows of stars.

Dowler was a bachelor. He was a man of about thirty-five. He was sensitive and loved civilized things—music, books, good food, and comfort. His house on the lake bore eloquent testimony to all this; but, if he wanted civilization, why come to Africa? He lived by the great lake with a certain royal abandon. He had four handsome, well-dressed African servants, who were obviously devoted to him and he to them. He watched over them with a solicitude remarkable in one so young. The more I got to know Michael, the clearer became my impression that he gave these children of African nature the consideration and affection he would have liked to give his own dark, unfulfilled self, only centuries of so-called European civilized values prevented him from doing this. We all have a dark figure within ourselves, a negro, a gipsy, an aboriginal with averted back, and, alas! the nearest many of us can get to making terms with him is to strike up these vicarious friendships with him through the black people of Africa.

We talked late into the night alone on the veranda. Michael assured me he had always wanted to go on the Nyika. It drove him nearly mad to wander up and down the low, hot, malarial plains at its base, infected with sleeping sickness, and month after month to watch the cool, purple flanks of the cloud-capped wall, feeling unable to escape up them. This was just the opportunity he wanted. Alan had made him free to do as he pleased, and if I would let him, he would love to come with me. The great question was bearers. But he himself was out in the bush most of the time and was therefore known to them far and wide. They seemed to like him and trust him. He never had any difficulty getting any. Would I let him try to raise a party for us?

I agreed to this as it made good sense. I would spend one day with him to complete arrangements and then hurry back to Msusi, pick up my tents and supplies, and rejoin him as quickly as I could.

We were up early the next day. Below on the lake shore the sun shattered the night and coolness in one quick blow. At one minute it was dark and cool, and the next the sun came roaring like a lion over the top of the far, purple Livingstone range on the eastern shore of Nyasa, and at once it was light and hot.

Before breakfast Michael had his two headquarters askaris, Harneck and Karramba, summoned to his room.

They were two young yet old soldiers, both of the King's African Rifles. Harneck was a good, solid, handsome peasant type, a stout African yeoman who, Michael said, could be relied on absolutely, though he was slow and too gentle. Karramba, who had something mercurial, almost Latin or Spanish about his appearance, was quick, clever, and brilliant, but a little cruel and at times not at all reliable. Michael kept them both because together they made a whole; apart they were inadequate. In a few minutes they had their orders and were packing up to set out into the bush for bearers.

"I have given them five days," Michael said, "to get us forty-five bearers."

After breakfast we got into Michael's car and drove fifty miles along the road by the lake to call on Bwamantapira, the greatest of the African lakeside Chiefs, whose authority stretched far back into the foothills of the Nyika itself. We came to Bwamantapira's village late in the afternoon. I do not know if he understood a word we said to him. He was dragged almost to the door of his small mud bungalow by a young wife and two handsome little black boys, and stood there in a daze, a fat, handsome man, swaying on his feet, dead drunk, agreeing amiably to all we said.

The dark overtook us on the way back, but it was preceded by a clear and unbelievably tender twilight. Michael had been out in the bush with his gun when it came. He had stopped to go after some guinea-fowl we had seen flying back from the lake to roost in golden trees. They seemed in the sunset glow to be covered with blue and silver sequins, with little scarlet scimitars over their dainty heads. The moment I saw them I knew Michael would not be able to resist following them. He was gone about twenty minutes. Meanwhile I sat by the side of the road and listened to the night symphony of the bush tuning up.

Fifty yards away a little duiker doe stepped out of the bush, looked at the car for about a minute, with the most arch and innocent surprise, and then stepped delicately back into the bush. Ten minutes later a large lion with a long black mane walked out purposefully at the same place and, without looking right or left, disappeared into cover on the far side. Near at hand three Franklyn partridges rose up in noisy hysteria. High overhead an eagle flew slowly by on ponderous wings, the pink afterglow burning on its feathers and glinting off a long silver fish in its talons. The night birds, lakeside frogs and crickets, gathered the scattered sparks of sound together and sent up into the silence a flame of evening song and praise. I was sorry when Michael ended the moment by stepping quietly out of the bush.

I told him about the lion. "Oh!" he said, with hardly a show of interest, "I expect it must be that fellow I nearly ran down with the car, just about here, the other night."

We dined that night with the District Commissioner, Peter Gracey, and his wife Joan. The light had gone long before we reached their house. As we walked through long lake grass up the track, to a shrill crescendo of night and water noises, we could see from far off their house-boy at the entrance waving a lantern to guide us. As we approached we heard a new sound—a sound of European music. The Graceys were playing their gramophone. It had a remarkable tone, and as we came nearer still we distinguished clearly the St. Matthew Passion of Bach.

I was instantly and profoundly moved by it. Not only was it so completely unexpected, but in that setting it sounded such a true, unfaltering statement of what is best in our complex European system of values. As I listened to the singing getting louder I felt that Bach's Passion was almost our justification. It seemed to give meaning to our being there by the dark lake, near the heart of that man-indifferent continent.

The voice of the crickets and the noise of the bush appeared to recede before the ordered advance of that silver, clear and unambiguous sound, and the night to let the great chorus rise unimpeded to the stars.

We sat talking with Peter and Joan Gracey far into the night. I could write much about them and the life they led in Karonga. I would like to dwell on the detail of their lives, but one more incident must be enough. At some moment in the evening, I think it was after we had been listening to a gramophone record of T. S. Eliot, and those lines which, although written about a Cambridge in America, always remind me so much of London that they send a stab of homesickness through me:

> "*The winter evening settles down*
> *With smells of steak in passageways.*
> *Six o'clock.*
> *The burnt-out ends of smoky days.* . . ."

I then said to Gracey: "As I came up the track, listening to Bach on your gramophone, I could not help wishing that Livingstone too could have heard something like it when he walked by here."

He looked at me sharply for a moment and said: "I expect he heard the same thing, in other ways."

He went on to say that the more he knew the African, the more impressed he was by the fact that when Livingstone died his bearers carried his dead body for hundreds of miles through hostile, dangerous country to the coast. It was a deed so remote from their normal state of being that he never ceased to wonder at it. Years ago he had met a very old native who remembered seeing Livingstone standing in the lake washing. When he lathered his head, the old man said, they all ran away because they thought he was a wizard taking his brains out. Yet with all that sort of superstition and ignorance about him, Livingstone captured their imagination to such an extent that, dead, he still urged his servants on. This was the real measure of the quality of his greatness.

Certainly, as I listened in my bed that night to the waves

on the shore, and recalled my first sight of the lake, I could understand as I had never done before how Livingstone could be both such a God-drunk and lake-intoxicated person. Having looked that wide land full in the face and seen those waters in their great frame of mountain and incalculable sky, it is not hard to realize how a search for them could easily be identified with a search for God.

I left Karonga before dawn the next day. As we now knew the road, we travelled fast, Peaches and I taking turns at the wheel. At four in the afternoon I was back at Msusi. Grantham was away with the General, but had left his house warm and open for me. I picked up my tents, blankets, cooking pots, ropes, petrol and food supplies. The jeep looked like a Christmas tree on wheels.

The next day we left again at dawn, and slept that night at Deep Bay on the lake with a hospitable trader at the depot of the African Lakes Corporation. We were back in Karonga soon after 9 a.m. and found the first bearers coming in.

Michael was delighted with the way things seemed to be going. The five days were not up until the following evening, but already eleven sturdy young bearers had come in and were being fed in the kitchen yard, seven of whom he knew from previous journeys in the bush.

We spent a busy day organizing our loads.

In the afternoon I did a round of the few small Indian stores in Karonga. I bought up almost their entire supply of blankets as well as a good quantity of salt, which we intended using as money in the hills, where it is very scarce.

Just before sundown Michael and I walked to the lake shore through green-gold papyrus grass shoulder-high and tasselled with seed. As it swayed in the slow breath of the evening air it seemed to spike and splinter the light between us and the sun.

The lake, in spite of its dense population of crocodiles, was full of black people washing. Some young girls, after coming out of the water, started to dance on the shining foreshore. They carried scarlet, yellow and brown wraps which, as they leaped and ran, they wove and unwove round their slim naked bodies. Some long, heavy, dug-out canoes, those black ships of Africa, were drawn up high on the beach, and several fishermen sat beside them in the amber light mending their nets, serenely continuous in their antique occupations. The waves of the lake pounded briskly, and urgently, at their feet, but they worked on unheeding.

Far away across the blue waters, on the threshold of Tanganyika, the mountains were purple and gold, their volcanic crevasses running full to the brim with the lava of the sun. It might easily have been a moment set for a meeting between Nausicaa and Odysseus on the Mediterranean shore, but, alas! it had to serve only as a moment of farewell in my own frantic little coming and going.

When we got back to the house, thirty bearers, all young and strong, were there. They made a good sight round their fires that night, and their lively conversation scattered a certain excitement on the air.

But there was a slight set-back the next day. Karramba came in just before lunch, dead-drunk, and with no bearers. I thought Michael's slim frame would burst with rage. He fined Karramba a month's pay, de-moted him, and straight away sent him on a fifty-mile journey to Bwamantapira with a letter asking the Chief to produce ten more bearers for us by the following evening.

We put Harneck in charge of our thirty-five bearers, and gave him one of my guns and some ammunition. We distributed two blankets to each man. They had not expected it and their delight was real and deep. They spread the blankets in the sun, waved them about their heads and filled the air with girlish cries of delight. It was astonishing, the sensitive, maiden-like sounds these husky black bodies suddenly emitted.

Michael then ordered them to take up their loads and

with these on their heads and their hands swinging free,
one by one they marched out of the yard with a glad will,
fell into a single file, singing in a well-calculated rhythm to
their long strides, and passed out of sight, the dust raised
by their feet rising like a swarm of golden bees into the
afternoon air.

We followed on by car the next day and joined them at
Deep Bay not far from Bwamantapira's village. The old
Chief himself was on the roadside to meet us. He had
made an effort to sober up and stood with two red-hatted
messengers of his court, waiting erect with immense dignity. He had great charm, knew it, and used it effectively
on us. He had received Michael's message, and said we
could count on him to produce bearers early the next day.

We camped that night by a heavy, black tree. I have
seldom seen a tree of a thicker and darker green. It was full
of bats and it seemed deeply dyed with their essence, and
drenched and dripping with their smell and matter. But it
stood on the only level ground, so we had to stay near it.

We had a wonderful view of the lake. It made a perfect
deep bay here, with the bush standing tiptoe in the lake
surf. Not far out from the shore five sharp pinnacles of
rock, stained white with bird droppings, burned with a
dull phosphorescent glow all through the night. We heard
the lake all night long, and at one moment a posse of
hippopotami who went huffing, puffing and snorting by to
raid the native gardens inland.

Our bearers were tired. They had come fifty miles in
about thirty-six hours. But we insisted on their getting into
our camp drill at once. We made them pitch their tent,
taught them how to make their tea, and rationed their rice
and sugar. By eight o'clock the camp was fast asleep.

# Chapter Twenty

WE broke camp at eight o'clock the following morning. Our bearers were still rather disorganized and we could not get going earlier. Bwamantapira's ten bearers arrived just as we struck tents. They came reluctantly, almost prodded on by the messengers of his court. They looked a sulking bunch so we allowed them no time either for feeding or feelings, but gave them their loads and sent them off ahead of us with the dependable Harneck and the rest. Trouble on these occasions, one knows from bitter experience, never occurs in front but always collects at the back.

The track now led us due west, through a low marshy plain, away at right angles from the lake shore. The Papyrus grass rose high over our heads and we had no view except an occasional glimpse of a purple wall of the remote Nyika.

It was hot, and we were glad to make the most of the moments when we had to stop to ask directions of passing natives. Our bearers were out of sight. Only Karramba, now thoroughly ashamed of himself, Michael's two servants, the cook and house-boy, draped in lamps, fats and pans, were with us.

At first we passed many natives, all sorts of small settlements of little mud and straw huts, discreetly and respectfully tucked into the shelter of some rise in the plain. But after twelve miles or so of steady walking all signs of settlement disappeared, and we saw no one. I was delighted when this happened, felt we really were on our journey and nearly sang for joy. I saw Michael suddenly give Karramba a cigarette and I knew he was feeling as I did.

After three and a half hours' steady walking we came

out of the grass and started a gentle climb on to higher ground. The bush came back, a pale, sallow, shimmering bush, full of sunlight and tentative apologetic shadow. From then on it stayed with us until about four in the afternoon, when we reached the fields and clearing of a little village, called Nkalanga. We had done about twenty miles from the lake shore and decided to call it a day.

The Umfumo of the village was already waiting for us, our bearers sitting expectantly round him, hopeful of our decision. He guided us to a magnificent level camping site under three vast, wild fig trees. There was both shade and space, and in a few minutes the loads were undone, the tents going up, the water and wood being fetched, latrines being dug, and the Umfumo himself came in to see what food his village would like to sell us. We said he was to find, if he could, an ox for the bearers. They had learnt their lesson well and the camp was organized much more quickly than the night before.

We were in the midst of our tea when the Umfumo returned, followed by a procession of women carrying trays of food on their heads, and these in turn were followed by an old man leading a young bull. Michael explained that it was extremely rare for the natives ever to have oxen, and began to bargain.

I say we bargained, but that is a hard word for what took place. As we looked at those thin, friendly, black faces, so delighted to have the monotony of their lives broken by our visit, neither Michael nor I had any desire to bargain. What we did was to instruct Harneck, the sober, reliable peasant, to agree with the sellers on a weight of salt, and then we doubled the quantity. As a result the village became, for that afternoon and evening, an extraordinarily happy place. Everywhere people suddenly started singing and smiling to themselves.

We bought fresh mealies, ground tapioca root, sweet potatoes and beans for the bearers, some eggs and a fowl for ourselves, and then slaughtered the bull. At least the bearers slaughtered it with a huge primitive delight. They leaped at it, pulled it down in the dust and promptly cut its throat without a squirm, smirk or shudder, feeling nothing apparently but a warm glow of anticipation at the meal in front of them.

While all this went on, I took my gun, some soap and a towel, and walked two miles along the track to the bed of the Fuliwa river. The sun was already behind the Nyika, the shadows were long and dark.

I could not see the Nyika itself for I was up against the foothills, but the river, the Fuliwa, or Wouwe as it is also called, rises there. Here it cut a deep gorge in the hills, and brought with it the cold, heavy, densely-packed air which so unmistakably came from high mountain-tops. The water, as I bathed, felt like ice after the heat of the plain, and although I told myself again that cold was relative, I was glad we had taken all those precautions for the carriers.

Somewhere up the gorge, so old Bwamantapira had told us, there was a track of sorts leading up to the Nyika. I could see no sign of it. It looked in that light as if our journey might be a desperate business.

I got back to camp in the twilight, to find Michael feeding the Umfumo with castor oil out of a bottle from our medicine chest. He made a little gesture of mock dismay and said: "I can't give him enough. He has nearly finished the bottle."

The news that the medicine chest was out soon went round, and the bearers crowded in on us from all sides. This was to become a daily scene in our camp and I often think back on it with real pleasure.

Michael dressed all the wounds and scratches, and many ugly festering things as well on those bare feet, felt the pulses, and administered according to need paludrine or M. & B., Epsom Salts or aspirin.

The native faith in the magic of white medicine was boundless, and at times they would pretend to be ill just in order to have some.  Whenever a pretender was detected and sent away, the good humour with which he took his exposure was only equalled by the delight of the by-standers.

With the slaughtering of the bull and this administration of medicine round the fire, we felt that our journey to the Nyika began to acquire a spiritual as well as a material shape.  It now possessed an idea and an emotion that belonged only to itself and which, however slight, would never exist again in quite the same way.  It was a deeply satisfying feeling, and I said to Michael:

"You know, I think we shall be all right now.  They are not a bad lot."

"I shall feel happier," he answered, "when we are deeper into the hills and away from all villages.  This is the last one near the lake, thank goodness!"

"The test will come to-morrow," I told him, and described what I had seen of the gorge.  "The only bearers who worry me a bit," I concluded, "are Bwamantapira's bunch; they look very dissatisfied."

He nodded and pointed to where one of the lakeside bearers, a huge, brawny, ill-tempered man, was addressing some of the others. We had already noticed him and christened him Jo'burg Joe.

"I don't think he will cut any ice with my Karonga lads, though.  There are only ten of his bunch, and at a pinch we might scrape through without them," Michael said.

The sight of the camp as a whole was reassuring, too. The bearers had now formed little groups and were grilling their meat round large open fires.  All sorts of visitors were coming in from around.  The conversation was brisk and lively and the laughter gay and carefree.  They recover very quickly from fatigue, these native sons of Africa. When they lined up for their evening pay, all trace of weariness seemed to have dropped from them.

Over dinner the bearers borrowed a drum from the

village. They discovered that they had one of the most famous drummers of the Northern Province in their midst —a man who had once drummed at a feast for seventy-two hours without stopping. He warmed up the drum, took his time and did a few trial runs on it, but nobody's heart was in it yet, and in Africa drum and audience must be as one. This drummer was obviously an artist; he felt instantly that his audience was not yet ready, not yet united within itself, and he made no attempt to force any real drumming on it.

Michael and I were eating outside our tent because it was still warm, and watched all this with interest. We were half-way through our meal when a black man stepped suddenly out of the bush and advanced into the flickering fire-light.

He was a strange-looking figure, quite different from the lakeside people. He was short, stocky, immensely broad-shouldered, with great muscles to the calves of his legs. He had broad feet with toes widely splayed apart. His clothes were in rags. He carried a large earthenware pot on his head, a long broad spear in the right hand, and had a fearless, independent look in his eyes. His skin, even in that fire and lamp-light, looked a clearer black than any of our people's.

I heard someone exclaim: "Auk! A Mpoka."

A thrill of interest went through the camp. The talking stopped. Everyone looked at the newcomer.

"I think he is from the Nyika," Michael whispered, and shouted for Karramba, who came at the double. Then they started a long conversation, at the end of which Karramba told us that the stranger was indeed a Mpoka, and that he lived in the hills just underneath the lip of the Nyika. He had come down to sell a pot of honey; would we like it? The season had been bad in the hills, and he needed salt and food.

There must have been forty pounds of wild honey in that pot and he asked only ten shillings for it. Karramba wanted to bargain, but we waved him aside and gave the man fifteen shillings.

We inquired if he would like to stay with us as a guide, but he shook his head and with the same independent air stepped back into the bush and vanished.

A terrific buzz of conversation broke out at his disappearance. The Mpokas are the only real mountain folk in Northern Nyasaland. There are few of them, and some say that they are either a dying race or vanishing into the greater tribes of the plain. To this day they cling to the high ground where they were driven by the Angoni, Henga and Arab slave traders of a century or more ago. There they cultivate a few remote valleys with difficulty, and eke out a precarious subsistence by collecting wild honey and selling it in the plain below.

There is no honey like it, I believe. It has a royal, antique flavour, a wild, sharp, stinging, uninhibited sweetness all its own, and it finds a ready sale. For it the Mpokas are welcome in the plain, though they themselves are viewed with a somewhat superstitious awe. They are believed to possess magic powers, the secrets of life and death, and the ability to change themselves into hyenas and leopards. They are, moreover, the metal-workers and the armourers of that world. Their steel is locally renowned. All the Mpoka men carry magnificent long, broad spears, which are as much a symbol of their craft as a weapon for their defence. Still deep in the African heart is the belief that the gift of the metal-worker is a gift from the hands of ancient gods. Moreover, the mistrust the people of the plain feel for the unknown Nyika is inevitably projected on the Mpokas as well.

The Mpokas for their part have no love of the people down below. They resent and distrust them of old, and keep their distance with a jealous and revengeful suspicion. I do not want to exaggerate these things, but the sharp interest aroused in our camp by this visitation out of the night was most marked.

Even the cynical Karramba watched our visitor go with some disapproval, and, making a wry face, said loudly for all to hear: "He says we have a long way to go to-morrow and would have done better not to come."

The heart went out of the drumming after that, the fires were allowed to sink into their coals, and the camp soon slept.

In the early morning the Umfumo accompanied us to the Fuliwa gorge and showed us where we could cross on a tree felled over it. Our bearers went over easily, as though they had done it all their lives. The tree was grey with age and worn smooth with the rub of many feet. I hated crossing over. I never get used to that sort of thing, no matter how often I do it. Whilst anxiously seeking a hold for my feet, I find that glimpses of fast-running water far below make the task of balancing, with a rifle over the shoulder, seem almost impossible. I have never fallen over yet, but I always expect to do so at any moment. I waited until they were all across, and admired Michael's technique from firm ground. He got over his dislike of the process by putting Harneck in front of him and Karramba behind—presumably to catch him should he stumble. He would then put his hand on Harneck's shoulder, appear almost to shut his eyes, and walk slowly and unfalteringly, like a somnambulist, to the other side.

I followed after him with infinite care, trying in vain to look indifferent.

On the far bank we waved farewell to the Umfumo. He was a small, pinched person, with an inexpressible look of something beyond our understanding on his face. He looked sad, marooned and abandoned on the edge of the immense, shimmering bush. Then we started to climb and soon passed out of his sight.

The track, and it was the only one, so the Umfumo had said, was at first a clearly defined footpath; but, a mile or two up the gorge, it trailed away into little more than a goat track, old, broken and obviously very rarely used. We climbed with the sun on our backs, and as the morning advanced it became very hot and the bush thinned out so much that it scarcely protected us. Within an hour all the bearers sat down for their first rest. Michael and I sat among them, and talked to them.

They were cheerful, and better for their meal of the night before, but it was obvious to me that they had not got their second wind as yet. And we were only just in the mouth of the gorge; the worst was to come. We gave them ten minutes and started off again.

Within three-quarters of an hour they asked for another rest. The track was getting steeper, but as yet there had been no difficult climbing in the real sense of the word. I noticed that the sides of the gorge were encroaching upon us and that the sound of the Fuliwa, which we had not seen since crossing it, was becoming louder.

Half an hour later the bearers wanted another rest. They were breathing heavily and complaining of pains in their legs. They rested nearly half an hour this time. The river was now quite close, and roaring like a gale through the trees. We climbed steadily for about another hour and came to the stream.

The trees fell away from us, and we looked up two steep grass summits, rising high on either side of us into a sky so blue that it was almost black. About fifteen yards away the main stream went cascading in foam and thunder down the gorge, and on the edge of the track was a deep pool. The bearers dropped their loads and soon were all splashing in the ice-cold water. All this looked very attractive, but we were already biting deep into the day. No one knew when we should get out of that gorge; obviously we could not spend the night there.

I spoke to Michael. He called over his Askaris and we got going again. Only Jo'burg Joe staged a demonstration. He was the strongest of them all but now he wanted a longer rest, and swore at Harneck. Michael instantly walked down on him and told him to take up his load. All the bearers had stopped and turned round to watch, with tense potentially critical faces.

Michael looked Joe calmly up and down as if he were seeing him for the first time. "Take up your load and do as you are told," he said quietly, as if there was no possibility whatsoever of further disobedience. Joe stood up and went on.

Things went better for a while, until we had to cross the river again. The far bank was a steep, grass precipice about five hundred feet high. We had to get up it. I felt desperately sorry for the bearers. It was hard work getting myself and my rifle up.

When they came to the top, they were exhausted. What was even more discouraging, we found ourselves on an isolated pinnacle, in a world of similar pinnacles, hemmed in by enormous grass-covered summits beyond. There was supposed to be a Mpoka village here, but we saw no sign of it, and the afternoon was beginning to level itself out.

We went painfully up and down four or five of the pinnacles, sank up to our knees in mud and slime at their bottoms, and struggled slowly out again on the other side. At about four, when we had only an hour and a half of daylight left, at last I saw in front of us not a pinnacle but a long grass spur, running gold and green straight into the sinking sun.

Our bearers were now staggered out in a long irregular line up and down the mountain. By agreement Michael stayed with the rear, and I went in front.

Thinking that one good example was worth more than all the exhortation in the world, I led with a sturdy, cheerful Karonga lad; I had several times helped him on and off with his loads, and his bearing had impressed me from the start. We went up this spur steadily. If one is to be a good example one must not stop; the secret is to go on, steadily, inexorably, on and on. The Karonga lad was all that and more. His lungs were heaving like a blacksmith's bellows, but he did not hesitate. He never once stopped but slowly went up and up and on. At five we climbed out on to the spur, the slope levelled out and we stepped along quite fast through some sort of tall gold rye grass. The nearest bearer was coming slowly along below us and about a mile behind. At five-twenty we suddenly came over the far crest of the spur, and there, perched close to us on the edge of a deep valley, was a little Mpoka hamlet of four huts, with sufficient level ground round it for tents.

I made my companion drop his loads, climb up a knoll and shout back the magic words: "People, a village, a village."

His clear voice raised a protracted echo, and then from far away came a glad, confused acknowledgment, passed farther and farther back into the distance. Just then the sun went down.

The village was called Mwatangera and the Umfumo, a fine-looking, sturdy young Mpoka man, in a scarlet beret, came tearing up the slope to meet me. His bearing was respectful, but he was too excited to be dignified. He took me by the hand and led me to the village and introduced me to his old father, who was so old that I would not like to guess his years. His eyes, once black, had gone blue and dim like those of a very old dog. He held on to my hand with both his own and would not let go, tears rolling down his cheeks.

I told the Umfumo that the real government officer was coming on behind me and at once he set off at a fast, eager pace to meet Michael. I noticed there were only two other men in the village. The rest were all women and dozens of fat-bellied, naked, wide-eyed little children. The men had already sent the women to work. Shouting and laughing with excitement and delight, they were tearing down the steep slope to fetch water in the valley, bringing in firewood and setting out some of their meagre supplies of maize and beans for our food. Soon there were half a dozen fires going to guide the rest of our party in.

We needed those fires. Within half an hour of sundown the thermometer was only a few degrees off freezing-point. A cold wind began to blow down the valley from the Nyika. Michael and I were cold in our tents and put on our warmest clothes. He drank a couple of large brandies, I some of a refined Spanish sherry that he carried with him. When his cook brought us large mugs full of chicken soup and great helpings of chicken and rice, we were really ready for it all. It was our first meal since seven that morning.

We had come, I estimated, about fourteen miles, and climbed, not counting those heart-breaking pinnacles and other ups and downs, about six thousand feet. For our reward, here on our second day out, we were camping right in a great mountain gateway to the Nyika. But we had pushed our bearers dangerously hard. It was obvious, so intense was the cold, that we could not possibly have spent the night out in the gorge. Nevertheless they were at the end of their strength.

"We had better rest them a whole day here to-morrow," I said to Michael.

When we told them, a deep murmur of gratitude and approval went through the camp, and everyone continued eating with a new zest. But there was no drumming that night.

"This is a no-good village, Bwana," said Karramba, with immense scorn: "it has not even got a drum."

Even if there had been one, I am sure it would not have been used.

## Chapter Twenty-one

I WOKE up the following morning feeling profoundly depressed. It was a lovely morning. As far as I knew I had had a good, if somewhat cold night. We had done well. I had gone to sleep in the best of moods. It looked as if nothing could now prevent us from getting to the Nyika, an event contrary to the ill-suppressed expectations of the experts and authorities on the area. The bearers were all in a good mood, laughing and talking with the greatest vivacity round their early morning fires. There was every reason why I should be rejoicing, but there it was: against all reason, and against my will and the evidence of my senses, I was possessed by this feeling of depression, which would not let me be.

As soon as we had finished breakfast we summoned the Umfumo and Harneck. I took my rifle, and Michael his cine-camera, which the Umfumo and Harneck carried between them, and together we descended into the valley.

To the west there were three peaks facing our camp across the valley: Nkalanga Head which did a sort of eurythmic half-turn straight into the air; Mount Charo, staid, solid, and dependable as became the central peak; and Kasanga Head which performed its own steep melodrama on the left of the other two. They were all three just under eight thousand feet high. We chose the golden mean and went up Charo.

It was not a difficult climb. The morning was bright and clear, and whenever we stopped to look back we had a fine view of the broken gorge and valleys through which we had come, the plain all of a tremble, and the sparkling blue waters of Nyasa far in the background.

In two hours we were nearing the top, and then suddenly

we were given a most effective illustration of the power of the African sun. We had just turned round to look back when, without warning, an enormous black cloud of twisting and turning mist materialized in the blue, and poured straight down on our heads. It was only ten o'clock on a winter's morning, but already there had been time for the sun to draw enough vapour off the lake to wrap all those remote mountain-tops in a thick black shroud.

The Umfumo, his scarlet beret now going in front of us like a lit candle, seemed undismayed by the event, said it was always like that, and would clear by and by.

We were doing the last and steepest part of the climb when the mist came down, and I had reason to be grateful to it; for, though I could not tell why, my feeling of depression seemed to have translated itself into an unusual and sharp attack of vertigo. We were climbing along an almost vertical grass slope, about two thousand feet high. Had anybody slipped or stumbled he would, without doubt, have shot straight down to the bottom, for there was not a tree or boulder on to which to hold. As a rule I am fairly good on this sort of occasion; but to my dismay I was obsessed that morning by a feeling that I had taken myself too high and too far beyond my own strength and balance. Then, and to my great relief, the mist came down and removed all sense of height.

Once on top we sat down to wait for it to clear so that we could, as the Umfumo promised us, get our first view of the Nyika. Michael prepared his camera for the great moment. I put my compass at my side on Henderson's map. Harneck and the Umfumo sat, with the natives' instinctive good manners, behind and away from us, and talked ceaselessly in low, contented voices.

It was dark and very cold. An icy wind was moving with the mist over the summit. I lay down on my back in the grass. How sheltered one was, and how warm there! I snuggled into it as deeply as I could, almost like a Steenbuck, the antelope which so hates draughts and cold winds that it has become a great artist in finding shelter even in the bleakest of places.

I took out my little pocket-book to make a note of the height of Charo . . . and suddenly I saw that it was a Sunday, and noticed the date. Then it was as if a large double barn-door in the granary of my mind burst open, and my depression tumbled out into the full light of day.

It had happened on a Sunday, a lovely warm glowing day at the foot of the ten-thousand-foot Goenoeng Gedeh in Java. This was its "forgotten" seventh anniversary. I, or rather the contemporary "I" on its own special mission to Africa, had forgotten, as it had done several times before. But there is that in our blood which does not forget so easily; our hearts and our deepest minds have a will and a way of their own, and there are anniversaries they insist on keeping no matter what our conscious preoccupations.

It was always so with me, anyway, and I was unspeakably depressed until I acknowledged and observed this grim birthday within myself. Once I had fully, openly acknowledged it, things were better. For here was one of those sad friendships I have mentioned earlier, and because it was more relevant to my inward journey than the time or the place through which I happened to be moving, I must again hold out a hand of recognition to it.

We were a small, it seemed a condemned, group of British and Australian prisoners of war in Japanese hands. We were in an old Dutch jail for desperate criminals, at the foot of the Gedeh, one of the loveliest of Java's many volcanoes. It was a Sunday morning after a night of rain; I was sitting in the sun, shaking violently with malaria, and trying in vain to keep warm, when the Japanese sent for the senior R.A.F. Officer, Wing Commander Nichols,[1] and

---

[1] Wing Commander, now Group Captain, W. T. H. Nichols is still serving in the Royal Air Force which he joined many years ago as a boy. One day I hope to write a book about the prisons he and I shared and to make some acknowledgment of the debt that his country and thousands of prisoners-of-war owe to him. He was a great camp Commander. In the last war I saw courage of all kinds but none quite of the Nichols' quality. It was almost a

myself. When we presented ourselves they told us we were to parade a party of twenty-five officers, and N.C.O.s, at two that afternoon. That was all, nothing more.

Nick seemed relieved. I said nothing. I was certain I recognized the look in their eyes. I had been through it before, he had not. They were either going to kill us, or kill someone else for our benefit. But I said nothing, for I might be wrong. Only I prayed in my heart that if I were right my malaria would abate sufficiently for my shivering to stop. I would not like them to see me shivering and think I was afraid.

We paraded at two. I was still shaking violently with ague. We marched out of the gate through streets full of Dutch civilians pushing their children in perambulators or taking them by the hand for their Sunday walk.

We were marched four miles to a large sports ground. All the machine-guns were out; there were hundreds of troops about in steel hats, with rifles and fixed bayonets. Hundreds of others, too, were laughing excitedly and flocking to the sports ground.

Yes, I had been right. It was to be a killing.

I said a prayer, silently, that my fever, that terrible shattering, malarial ague, might go. Instantly my body stopped shaking, and a lovely warm sweat broke over me.

"Look!" I said to Nick in utter and grateful amazement, holding out my hand. "My hand is quite steady now."

He smiled with approval and answered, "Good show!" His understatement was very English.

---

matter of routine with him. All day and every day it was with him, as much a part of him as the colour of his eyes or the shape of his head. Neither that courage, nor what is rarer still, his imagination, failed him or us in those long, grim, inarticulate years in Japanese prisons. When we were released I stayed behind in Java, but I happen to know that on return to England not one of our thousand-odd British prisoners-of-war needed rehabilitation—so unlike the prisoners returning from other theatres of war. I hope that someone, somewhere, in the R.A.F. has said to himself, "This is most unusual. How did this miracle occur?"

Already there were a thousand Dutch officers and men drawn up on the sports ground, and a similar number of Ambonese troops of all ranks. We marched our party in between them and faced about. Just opposite us, twenty yards away, two bamboo stakes were dug firmly in the ground.

"Look, you fellows," I said, or words to that effect, "it's going to be an execution, so hold on to yourselves and be prepared."

"Yes," said Nick, "I needn't remind you chaps who we are, and why we are here. Stand fast!"

We then saw the victims. I do not know their names to this day, but the manner of their going deserves a recording, even if it now cannot help them. One was a Eurasian, one an Ambonese. They marched jauntily and firmly on to the ground. The Eurasian was tied tightly to the two stakes; the Ambonese was made to kneel down in the grass in front of us, almost at our feet, and his hands were tied behind his back. One's first reaction was: "Thank God, not two of ours," and then, "Poor bloody, bloody devils."

The black muzzles of a dozen heavy machine-guns swung over towards us. A Japanese officer walked up to the Ambonese, who had long black hair. The officer lifted up his hair from his neck and dropped it over his eyes. Then he stepped back, drew his sword, measured his distance, stepped forward again, and smoothed the Ambonese's hair again. He repeated this cruel business backwards and forwards five times.

On the sixth, he raised his sword, yelled suddenly, deeply from his stomach like a man in a nightmare, leaped forward and cut the head off in one blow.

All round us the Dutch and Ambonese were falling in dead faints.

"Stand fast, chaps," Nick said.

A loud-speaker almost drowned his words.

"This man has been killed," it boomed at us, "because he has shown a spirit of wilfulness to the Japanese Army."

Three Japanese soldiers with fixed bayonets now lined up in front of the Eurasian. His body was stretched between the stakes as on a cross. Then the Japanese on the right uttered the same mindless, inhuman, aboriginal, solar-plexus scream as the first officer had done, and plunged his bayonet three times into the bound Eurasian, whose skin at the first plunge snapped like a drum. The next soldier, and then the next, repeated the performance; then all three turned about again, fell on their stomachs, and fired four volleys into the limp and sagging body of the Eurasian.

All this time our twenty-five men had stood fast, but the officer next to me, Ian Horobin,[1] though still on his feet, was dead to this world, a condition that did all honour to him. He, like the rest of us, was living out each last second with those two humble, nameless victims, and living them through with neither hope, nor pity, nor expectation for himself. But at the first bayonet-stab he winced, as though he himself had received the blow, and swayed on his feet. I put my arm round him and in that way managed to hold him up through the rest of the whole bloody business; and in this moment, for me, lies the real significance of that afternoon. For as I put my arm round Horobin, a stranger, in order to support him, I felt to my utter amazement how near he was to me. There seemed

[1] Ian Horobin, formerly Conservative Member of Parliament for Southwark, when war broke out abandoned politics for service in the R.A.F. After the capitulation of the Allied forces in Java he made an attempt to break away and join me in the hills of Bantam; but, as a result of this, he fell ill, was captured by the Japanese and imprisoned. Because he resolutely refused to answer the questions put to him about me and other matters, he was sorely beaten-up and ill-treated by his captors and was in a very poor state of health when I too was bundled into prison with him many months later. But his spirit was indomitable and we all brought away with us a generous store of the wise and witty sayings with which Horobin enlivened our days in jail.

He wrote a most moving poem about this execution called "Java Sunday". We buried it carefully lest it should fall into Japanese hands. After the war I kept a company of Japanese prisoners digging for it for a week but we never found it again and alas, Horobin can neither remember it nor has the heart to re-write it. And in a sense this is not necessary. The poem is being lived out in another way, for to-day Horobin puts all his great qualities of mind and spirit unreservedly into the running of the Mansfield House University Settlement for Boys in the East End of London.

to be no barrier between us; we might have been the same person under the same skin; and, in spite of the dreadful circumstances of the moment, a tremendous warmth and reassurance welled up within me, like wine and song. All sense of isolation, all my restless, seeking self, my desperate twentieth-century awareness of isolation and doom vanished. I was out of it all in a flash, and far beyond in a world of inseparable nearness. This, I knew, was true: this nearness of him to me, of me to him. It was the heart of reality. That was how we all were, close to each other, if only we would allow ourselves to be so. With a singing sense of deliverance from unreality, from the prison of myself and my surroundings, I resolved that in the years to come I would never forget this moment. I resolved that if I lived—and I did not really care then one way or the other—I would try and carry this moment along with me in all that I did. Then Nick put out his arm to help Horobin, touched me, and I noticed that he, too, felt equally near.

That night, back in prison, we found a gloom as deep as night waiting for us. At first there was tremendous relief at our return, but as the news of the execution spread, the conviction grew that we should be the next victims. We summoned all the men to our regular evening service, Horobin read the lessons, and spoke to them as though he were a prophet down from a mountain in Palestine. That helped, but they were still depressed. I still had malaria, and was shaking again with the ague that had returned as soon as I re-entered the prison, but I knew I must do something to help the men through that night and out of their gloom.

Africa came to my rescue. I talked to them about the animals of Africa for two and a half hours; about the bush, the plains, the great free mountain-tops and immense skies, about a life that was a continuous trek, a journey without walls or streets to hem it in. The sense of doom, the transmitted memory of the killing in the afternoon, receded,

H

thanks to that re-created vision of my boyhood in Africa, and before the night was over our jail rang with laughter over the antics of baboons and elephants, lion and rhinoceros. I had realized then how deep, how life-giving and strengthening was this vision of Africa in my blood; that possessing this, and my knowledge of our nearness to each other, I could travel to the end of the world and time.

Suddenly I sat up, on the top of Charo, with so keen a feeling of happiness and release, that tears came to my eyes. It was still dark. Michael was still at his camera, the Umfumo and Harneck still talking. I could not have been more than a minute or two, reliving that moment seven years before. But the good of it was mine. The rest receding.

I lay back on the grass: the mountain seemed to take a firm, a friendly grip of my back. It, too, felt unbelievably near and sustaining. It seemed as if through me and through its great, strong heart, and right down to the centre of the earth, ran the axis on which the wide world turned through space and time. I had a vision of the universe and myself, in which circumference was reduced to a mere mathematical abstraction, and in which all was Centre; one great unfailing Centre, and myself, in the heart of Africa, in the heart of the Centre.

Yes, if we were as close and near one to the other, what then kept us so obviously, painfully and dangerously apart? The man on the stake, the headless Ambonese, Horobin, Nick and I were conceivably near to one another, but what could have been farther from that one-ness than the Japanese? It seemed so clear to me that morning. The distance between them and us was the distance of their unreality; just as the distance between us all to-day is created by our unreality. Those Japanese did not know what they were doing. They thought they were doing something which they were not doing. They gave their victims a fine, romantic military funeral—and what more could men want? They thought they were performing their duty nobly, beautifully and justly. Yet they were doing the opposite and doing it because their awareness of themselves, and of life, was inadequate. For this unreality starts in an incomplete awareness of ourselves; it starts in the elevation of a part of ourselves at the expense of the whole. Then, out of this dark gorge which we have allowed to open up between the two halves of ourselves, out of this division between the Europe and the Africa in us, unreality rises up to overwhelm us.

Evidence is everywhere that the great tide of unreality is running full. The human being, the natural person has never had so little honour from life and from himself as today. He is imprisoned in theories, in petrified religions, and above all, strangled in his own lack of self-awareness.

There is murder about. The air is foul with the stink of rotting corpses. But murder does not begin on the battlefield. There, in a sense, is the least of it. The murder is in our hearts, in our deeper selves, and no vicarious adventures in the footsteps of Holmes, Wimsey, and Poirot will let us off. The murderer is powerful and respectable. He has churches, sciences, trade unions, political movements and dictators on his side, and he does not know his crime. He has a clean morning face, is well-spoken, has good manners and fine clothes. He sits with the judges and their laws are for him. He is good at getting himself increased wages, more afternoons off, better houses and finer gadgets, which are more and more ingenious in order to disguise the triviality of the service they render.

There is no great harm, perhaps, in all this. But what of his brother on the other side of the fence, the dark Siamese twin on the other side of the gorge, the Caliban tucked out of sight on the stormy side of the isle, the despised African far behind these blue escarpments? We murder him or are murdered by him from time to time, but can we blame our dark brother? If we murder him for virtue, why can't he kill for survival?

For those who care to look, the sad, secret presence of

this killing is in all our bright twentieth-century eyes. The Molotovs of this world, the multi-millionaire, the quick, intolerant Puritans and one-eyed surgeons carry the secret of their own urge to murder on their faces, for all their unawareness of it. It is only unreality that keeps us apart, that kills and murders and composes hymns of praise of Siberian concentration camps and metropolitan profiteers.

Yet this need not be. There is room for both, for Ariel and Caliban, for Cain and Abel, there is room for all, without murder, at the Centre, in the heart, without circumference. Could fair and dark, night and morning, but understand the language they speak to each other across this dark gulf of unawareness, they would fall into one another's arms and embrace.

I repeat, only this awareness is true. And in this moment of reality the human being is neither fearful nor cringing. He does not mind how much he is asked to do, or how dangerous it is, if only it is something single, whole, complete and sufficient for his full self. He is greater than any dictator, factory or trade union. He is a mighty and heroic atom.

Any vision of himself or of life which does not acknowledge this, either kills or is killed. For there, in the heart, man's own dark aboriginal courage makes him free, his humbleness before the mystery of his being brings awareness, awareness makes him whole and wholeness gives him love. But merely to offer him increased wages, religious, political and scientfic soporifics is to breed more murder. Give him a horse, give him a spear and bring out the dragon!

"I think," Michael called out to me suddenly, "the mist is going to break."

I sat up and opened my eyes. Indeed it was less dark, and along the edges of the other summits the mist was beginning to lift, a silver light running like a pentecostal fire all along the sombre ridges. For a few minutes we had a view that uplifted us beyond measure.

World beyond world we saw, a tremendous, rolling, fold-ing country, clean, golden, grass-covered, rising like some Olympian pastoral symphony to a dark blue ridge, an Atlantic roller of land, fifteen miles west of us. In all the folds there appeared to be water, in all the bottoms dark-green copses, but no sign of people or human habitation of any kind.

"Bwana," said the Mpoka Umfumo with a smile as if this was his own work. "The Nyika, but the best Nyika, it is on the other side of the ridge."

As he spoke the mist came down again. We waited, but it refused to budge.

Released from myself, my eyes looked round the summit and were held by a purple glow in the green-gold grass.

I got up and went towards it. The summit was covered with wild irises, with lovely, proud spikes of purple flower. Everywhere there were small, glowing, delicate, precise flames of purple. They stood erect and undismayed, heral-dic in the mist and wind. The grave, lowered head of the African plateau could not have understood the vision of chivalry they evoked. For they seemed to point a way, to presuppose a flame without fear or reproach—or was that but another fancy of a fevered heart?

On my way down I picked an armful to put in our tents, and that night I dreamed a dream. I tell it here, not be-cause I have a theory about dreams, but because as a child I was profoundly impressed one night when my grand-father read out to us that passage from Genesis beginning: "And Joseph dreamt a dream and told his brethren and they hated him for it." It seemed to me then that there was a lesson one could learn from dreams. Here it is for what it is worth.

I dreamed I saw my father and mother standing to-gether smiling in our garden at home. I did not remember ever seeing them like that. It was morning. The sun was shining. They were admiring a rose. The rose was white and the rose was on fire.

## Chapter Twenty-two

THE dawn the next morning was one of the loveliest I have ever seen. There were a few clouds over the lake and these were soon in flames. Standing at the door of my tent in the cold, pure air, it looked as if a green fleet of ancient ships, their sheets filled with fire, were plunging forward to battle. A happy murmur rose from the fires where the bearers squatted on their heels; now well fed they were keen to be away from that cold, drumless, foreign Mpoka hamlet.

Michael ordered the bearers to take up their loads and start at exactly eleven minutes to eight. Karramba took the lead and they went slowly down into the valley and up the other side, through the immense gateway between Charo and Kasanga.

They seemed to me to be taking the slopes in too direct a fashion, too steeply. They would have done better, I thought, to make use of the contours, but I did not worry unduly, because their behaviour was characteristic of the African. His sense of distance is not ours, and in any case his life is so surrounded with difficulty and trouble, and ups-and-downs everywhere, that he does not really believe he can ever get round things. So he would as soon go through with them and get them over and done with as quickly as possible.

We climbed on slowly from one valley to the next. We came across a tiny hamlet of three huts where the bearers all quickly sat down to rest and drink water. Then a black cloud suddenly materialized in the blue above, and poured down into the valley. In a few seconds we were in a thick fog and bitterly cold.

Fortunately after a time the going became easier. The

mist spoilt our view but we were plainly no longer struggling up and down mountain crests. The Umfumo said we were going over the eastern ridge of the country we had seen from Charo—not the true Nyika, he was anxious to add, but part of the Nyika none the less. What we were able to see, though, was superb African Cotswold country, lovely grass slopes, steep certainly but wonderfully free of trees and stone. Only tucked into the corner of each fold was a neat dark green copse, a Druid circle of sombre wood. In each bottom was a deep, clear, still stream, and again no people.

We saw no game, but according to the Umfumo the woods were full of leopard and wild pigs.

We did about twenty miles in the mist and at half-past four in the afternoon found ourselves on the edge of another deep valley. There was no question of it being another fold. On our left I could just see the bulk of what was Nganda Head, a mountain 8,600 feet high, and the highest point on the Nyika; and on our right a dark mass rising into the mist, which, the Umfumo told us, was Wendenganga. According to my map we should now be in the centre of the Nyika; but that valley, that unmarked cleft between the two peaks, was certainly no Nyika.

We went steeply down into it for about two thousand feet, and came to a small hamlet called Nkanta. It consisted of four tiny mud igloos, not huts but little mud beehives, occupied by another dim old man, four strapping young women and an immense brood of children. They received us as if we were angels. The old man said he had not seen a white face for twenty years, and he followed Michael round like his own shadow.

We pitched our camp there for the night. The bitter wind was bearing down the valley. It was cold, and we had to drive the bearers hard to put up their tents before dark. All they wanted to do was to make a fire and get round it. However, we soon had the camp staunchly pitched and well pegged down, like a ship with battened hatches and iron scuttles clamped on, against the night. Before this, we had built enormous fires and issued generous rations. It was as well we did. It blew a gale before morning, and the temperature went down to within a degree of freezing-point.

The wind dropped with the coming of the sun the next day. We packed up early, and travelling along the valley did close on twenty-five miles. We passed two small hamlets, both of which turned out their one old man, their four or five women and broods of children, who danced round us and sang and clapped their hands from one end of their clearings to the other. At each hamlet we stopped to exchange news and to leave a small present of salt. They were people who had no contact with the outside world whatsoever, and whose gratitude was very moving.

All the way, in spite of my map, this cleft not only persisted but widened. The flank of the Nyika on our left became sheer precipice with unexpected cliffs of grey stone round the top. On our right and behind us it swung away in a wide curve towards the distant lake. About four in the afternoon the left flank of the Nyika too was turned.

We had come, as far as I could judge, to its northernmost point, and there hard by was the village of Njalowe. I had been told it would be in the heart of the best of the Nyika. It was nothing of the sort. It was in the heart of the bush far down at its feet. But it was a real native village with quite a fair-sized population, and it gave us a tremendous reception.

The people of Njalowe must have spotted us coming miles away, though how they managed to do this I do not know. The Umfumo and his elders met us several miles from the village and escorted us. A mile out, a party of about a hundred women came down the track to greet us. There was no pretence about all this, nothing forced, they were really glad to see us; it was a spontaneous act of welcome.

As soon as they saw us they raised a clear, bell-like warbling, yodelling cheer and came leaping and dancing towards us. All the way into the village they danced ecstatically round us and sang improvised songs of welcome with flawless, unselfconscious, glittering voices, clapping out the rhythm on their hands. There was nothing, no reservation, no qualification, no forethought between the desire to sing and the singing, the process was continuous and immediate.

I was quite certain, for my part, that I did not deserve such a Messianic reception, but I enjoyed every minute of it. I was fully convinced long before they led us into the village that we were really welcome. It is worth walking and climbing a long way to have that feeling. It is a good, healing, human feeling, and helps to melt some of the ice, and the calculation in our cold, de-humanized, limited-liability twentieth-century hearts.

Our camping site was already prepared for us, and food, firewood and water were all being fetched. There was no need to pitch any tents except our own, because Njalowe is so low down that it was warm, out of the wind and mist, and even at that late hour flushed with the full rays of the setting sun. A busy market sprang up round us.

No sooner had the women and girls seen us to our camping site than they dispersed, running and laughing happily along the village tracks. They were soon back again. Very dignified and serious now that they had business to do, and carrying great baskets of produce on their heads.

They brought mealies, fresh, ripe and stamped; beans, peas, sweet potatoes, sour milk, fowls, eggs and tapioca roots. We bought food for our bearers; they bought food for themselves. I am sure Njalowe had never had such a market. Finally, we bought a bull for slaughter in the morning.

We did this because I felt we could not move on until we had explored this unrecorded gap in the Nyika. I was desperately anxious to get on to the true Nyika myself, but the unexpected existence of this large wedge of unhealthy, low-lying, practically uninhabited country, in what I had hoped would be the northern end of the plateau, could not be ignored. Michael and I therefore decided that we would rest the bearers for another day and night and ourselves do some reconnoitring with the new Umfumo as our guide. We were quite certain that, with a bull to slaughter and eat, our bearers would come to no mischief in our absence. And also there was the drum.

When Michael and I came back from our bathe in a stream at the bottom of the village, Karramba met us with the news that Njalowe had a drum, a real drum, famous for its responsive tone. It could either boom like thunder or record the fall of a feather. If we stayed another night, they could have a real dance and do some proper drumming.

On the far side of the wide gap or valley in which Njalowe stands, there is a mountain close on eight thousand feet high, called Nkawozya. It has an impudent look about it, and seems to turn up the nose of its summit at whatever is around it.

I decided that the first thing was to find out what I could see from the top. Accordingly Michael and I, and the Chief, set off across the valley soon after the first light, taking with us Harneck, the indefatigable peasant askari, who had struck up a great friendship with me.

The Chief carried a magnificent broad spear, and a beautifully made snuff-box, shaped rather like a musketeer's powder horn. He stopped from time to time to help himself and pass the horn round with a royal hand. I think he had some Arab blood in him somewhere, and he wore a cloth like the Javanese Kaiang round his head.

On the way he told us that for miles around there were very few people. They hardly ever saw anybody from the outside world. Karonga was their nearest town, but it was several days' journey along a narrow lost track through the bush and plain. Many of his young men had to go into the world outside to find a living, and they did not all come back, or came back perhaps just to get a wife and then went away again. His whole community too was getting smaller.

We walked in this way up and down the steep folds in the valley to the base of the main peak of Nkawozya, doing in all about nine miles, in two and a half hours. We then climbed it without difficulty in about an hour and a half. The view from the top was most rewarding, in fact told me all I wanted to know.

To the north was Mpanda, another impudent peak slightly lower than Nkawozya, cocking a snook at the plain towards Karonga.

The real Nyika lay to the south of us; its northernmost point was hard by Njalowe, and although we could not see into it, we could see its great wall running south as far as the eye could reach. It was clear that the following morning we should have to climb up the steep grey peak immediately behind the village (it was called Chelinda by the natives), and then at last we should be in the country we had come to find.

I took some bearings to make sure and told Michael.

He gave a mock groan and said: "Oh God! must we climb out of this all over again? You know, I am beginning to feel about it as Moses must have done about the Promised Land. We keep on getting tantalizing glimpses of the Nyika but we never really get on it. Do you think we ever shall?"

While I worked on my bearings, I sat in the shelter of a rock out of the wind. Michael, some distance away, took a hundred feet of film or more. The view was tremendous. According to my map there should be bench marks on Nkawozya, but I could not find any. According to the Chief no European had ever climbed Nkawozya before.

I was sitting apart from the rest when suddenly, close to my left ear, there was a tremendous swoop and flutter of wings. An eagle brushed my head, seemed to snatch at my

compass which was all a-glitter in the sun, thought better
of it and sheered off.

"It's all right," I shouted to Michael who, startled, called
out to me; "it's all right. It's a good omen. The time you
want to be careful in mountains is when buzzards drive the
eagles off."

On our return journey, we heard every now and then,
from far off in the camp, a roll or two on the drum.  It was
evidently being warmed up for the night.  It is a slow and
skilled task getting an African drum up to the right temperature and texture.  Our drummer, who had such a great
reputation to confirm, was obviously starting in good time
and taking no chances.  But what struck me particularly
that day about the far-off drumming was its absolute ap-
propriateness to its physical and human setting.  I seemed
to have missed that point in my past.  But the drum is as
appropriate to Africa as the elephant's trumpet, the lion's
roar, the leopard's cough, or the first tap of thunder in a
dry summer, on a parched and shimmering horizon.

We were back in camp just before sundown.  It was full
of activity and a recognizable party excitement.  Everyone
was being very nice to everyone else, and quite unable to sit
still.  Karramba was everywhere.  The ox had been
slaughtered.  The bearers in twos and threes had raised
little grills of green wood, and were getting the coals up
underneath them for cooking their meat.  In the centre of
the bearers, talking happily to all and sundry, sat our
Umfumo in his scarlet beret.

When he saw us he at once came over and explained
gravely that he would have to leave us early in the morning.  He had come as far as his knowledge went, and could
not let his old father and his women stay alone any longer.
We said good-bye to him with real regret.

## Chapter Twenty-three

As the sun went down the women started coming in from the village. They wore their wraps now lightly folded round them and as they walked down the tracks, silhouetted against a bright red sky, they took on an ancient classic appearance.

Soon after dark the party began. I was standing with Harneck and a group of the bearers watching a large aeroplane, blazing with light in every window, coming up from behind and above Nkawozya. It was, I thought, the mail plane from Heath Row to Johannesburg; a machine that did seven thousand miles in thirty-six hours.

As we watched it go by, the stars became, for the first time, very distinct and clear. I was getting the native names for them when the drumming began in earnest. I was soon alone and I walked a little way up the crest towards the village so that I could see the whole camp at a glance. There was no dancing at first but only singing.

The singing was lusty and clear, with many voices in harmony, but it had, like all African tunes, an undertone of frustration and melancholy in it.

As far as I could make out they were singing about their lives, not as they had been once, or could be again, but as they were in their vast present, in their shimmering and parched monotony. They sang about their little fields of maize and corn, about how the women tilled them, and the pigs and baboons raided them till there was no sleep left for anyone in the villages, and no happy evenings round the drum, only a cheerless night-and-day vigil in the midst of their crops. And what for? So that their stomachs, those insistent, never satisfied stomachs, could be fed, and for no other glory or aim. And the drum at this point was

237

the stomach, was its solar plexus, its digestive system, its craving for more, more, more, its own blind, dead, monotonous means and end.

They sang about an African boy called Charlie to whom Capetown was magic, Johannesburg Eldorado, who left the village and never returned. They sang about their taxes, they sang about the Government they had never seen, they sang about us and this journey we had brought them on, and where and when was it all going to finish? Oh! the questions that drum asked, and did not pause to answer, but just went on and on bringing all back to its basic theme, this routine of birth, begetting and dying, set in the harsh, monotonous, parched routine of Africa, from which there is no escape and in which there is no change.

Life could be more and it could be less, it could be long or brief, it could go faster and it could be slower, but in its essence, in its heart there was no change, no hope of change ever, unless there could be—and could there?— some magic somewhere, some medicine that could redeem all?

If anyone wants to know the African heart he should listen to its drum as I did that night alone on the crest between the two frayed ends of my journey. It is entirely appropriate to its meaning. It, too, cannot change, it cannot alter its voice or tone, but by God, it can be fast or slow, loud or soft, long or short. It knows densities and rhythm but only one quality. It takes you so far, with a beating, straining heart, and then drops you and your excitement in the dust, because it cannot go beyond. But it can and does begin again.

I walked close and watched them dancing. In the flickering firelight the men and women, their dark faces absorbed in an expression beyond knowing, stood in two opposite rows. The drum began softly, and a quiver went through their bodies; the basic desire was born. The blood began to rise, to sing and thunder in their ears, the drum became their pulse, was in them, and set the hungry, the eager pace.

There was no pretence about it. There was no guilt, no sense of shame, only a great wide longing of the body to be one, to be free of the winter of separation; a longing of the fraction to be a whole. It was a necessity of the blood, and most innocent. The tiniest children were there, watching their fathers, mothers and sisters with wide-eyed approval, as they gave this orchestration by dance and drum of the physical movements of the sexual act.

When the excitement in the blood was so high that it could rise no higher, when the drum could go neither faster nor louder, this antique fever had its spasm. It was as if an electric spark leapt from one black head to another, a brilliant stream of lightning from one cumulus crest to another, and men and women leapt at each other, seized each other round the waist with frenzied hands, and went quickly, violently, like a tree shaking in a storm, through the motions of the act of love. And then the spasm left them. Was this all there was to it? Was there nothing beyond? After such frenzy was nothing changed? The drum died down to a low tap of slow despair. The bodies broke apart, shoulders sagged and feet trod a listless rhythm. A low musical wail, heart-rending to hear, burst from the bearers round the fire.

Time passed on. The fire in the heart, the glow of coals in the blood, sank low. Could it ever flare and flame again? The drum tapped on softly, hard to hear, but with the rhythm still just there. Black faces in the firelight stared sombrely, watchfully at their own flames of wood. The smell of burning meat rose like sacrificial incense in the dark, to appease what gods, what everlasting hunger?

Surely this could not be the end, this could not be all; they could and must try again. The drum rapped out a roll of warning, it drummed an imperious call to attention. The bodies became erect and then it all began once more. The same excitement. Perhaps this time it would be different. The drum went far, farther perhaps than drum had ever been before; the bodies twisted, the heart beat, as neither bodies nor heart had ever twisted or beaten before. It must be, it could be different. But was it? "Oh no! Oh no! Oh no!" the watching figures wailed round their burnt offerings at the flickering firesides. And again the prancing bodies, in the half-world between the night and the camp-light, fell apart, as if emptied of themselves, emptied of fire and hope.

This then is the great, the joyful and the tragic drama of the African's life: its glory and its humiliation. As far as they will take him, he follows the body and its interests across the gulf of our split natures into that dark country on the other side. He puts all his trust and faith in the splendour of his body, he encourages it to shake and convulse with desires of flame, and appetites so violent and clear that their satisfaction alone may become purpose and end enough. He is strong, brave, enduring and patient in their service, but at heart there is still this "Oh no! Oh, no! Oh no!"

It is not enough, there is a hunger still that escapes, that will not be satisfied. There must be something else, something more to give it, but what and how and where? Perhaps there is magic. Ah, he has tried that, and goes on trying it, but in the end the circle rounds on itself, leads the old trail back to the devouring stomach, the beating heart, to the world below belt and navel.

He belongs to the night. He is a child of darkness, he has a certain wisdom, he knows the secrets of the dark. He goes to the night as if to a friend, enters the darkness as if it were his home, as if the black curve of the night were the dome of his hut. How the ghosts of the European mind are warmed with memories of the African's response to the night. He does not really care for the day. He finds his way through it with reluctant, perfunctory feet. But when the sun is down, a profound change comes over him.

He lights his fire, he is at once happy and almost content, sings and drums until far in the morning. All would be well if there were not still his hunger. And what should he do about it?

We could tell him—we who have too much of the light and not enough of the night and wisdom of the dark. We could, but we will not because we are split against ourselves, we are infinitely prejudiced against the night.

Half the love we give ourselves would do for him; half for our bright morning selves, and half for him. It is enough for both: two halves for a whole, and the whole for both. Listen to his drum and listen to his wail, look how he goes with people like Michael and myself, cheerful, staunch, friendly and strong, on a journey he does not understand, to a place he distrusts. He would go anywhere we ask for half our love. There is no problem there.

It is an irony so characteristic of our basic unreality to blame the problem on him, to shoulder him with our fears and our sin, to call it a black, a native, an African problem. It is a striking, an effective, a plausible irony. But it is not true. The problem is ours; it is in us, in our split and divided hearts; it is white, it is bright with day. We hate the native in ourselves; we scorn and despise the night in which we have our being, the base degrees by which we ascend into the day.

I say this not to evoke emotion, to prove a theory, or to score a point in a special plea. I say it because I believe it is a law of life. It is as much law as the law of gravity. Defy gravity and you break your neck; outrage this law and you break your heart and lose your soul.

Scientists and judges have not the monopoly of laws. Euclid was an intuitive pattern before it became a textbook; Lucretius produced the atom whole out of his heart before it was split in a bomb on Hiroshima. The wholeness and the split, both, are within us.

But we have come dangerously late to this new awareness. We do not understand that we cannot do to others what we do not do to ourselves. We cannot murder and

kill outside without murdering and killing within. We turn
our hate on to the native, the dark people of the world,
from Tokyo to Terra del Fuego, because we have tram-
pled on our own dark natures. We have added to our unreality, made ourselves less than human, so that that dark
side of ourselves, our shadowy twin, has to murder or be
murdered.

Already there is the smell of murder approaching far off
in the sky over Africa. And this need not be, this is the pity
of it. If we could but make friends with our inner selves,
come to terms with our own darkness, then there would be
no trouble from without.

But before we can close our split natures we must forgive
ourselves. We must, we must forgive our European selves
for what we have done to the African within us. All begins
with forgiveness. Even the spring is a re-beginning because
it is sheer, utter forgiveness and redemption of the winter
and its murder of leaves.

Still the drumming went on. It did not vary except that
each repetition became louder, quicker, more insistent,
and the rush of man and woman at each other and then
clasping of each other became more and more frenzied.

Feeling as I did I couldn't face my tent. I climbed
higher up the crest. The night was very dark: there was
no moon, no pallid, half-way house of sun and earth about
with its cold mirrored unreality of reflection. The stars
were exceptionally bright and clear. They, too, seemed to
have taken up the beat of the drum. The sense of oneness
which that drum could create between itself and all that
belonged to the night passed all comprehension.

The Milky Way was superb, more like a track densely
strewn with daisies than its usual blur of misty light.
Orion, Vance's old hunter, club erect, jewelled belt
tucked tightly into his slim waist, seemed to be prancing
like a buck negro to the throbbing of the drum. Castor and
Pollux, the heavenly twins, Alfa Centauri, Sirius, the
watch-dog at that dark entrance through the Milky Way

into the greater night beyond; our own Jupiter, Mars and the inevitable Plough were all there, spear, bow, arrows and blade in hand. And away to the south where lay the Nyika, the land of to-morrow, a dark, pointed peak cut deep into the night. It was a night so clear that I had no difficulty in recognizing the full line of the great head of Chelinda. Immediately over it hung the Southern Cross.

As a Cross, I know it is not perfect. It is not symmetrical. But to love only perfection is just another way of hating life, for life is not perfect. And now, as I looked at the Cross, it seemed to hang over the proud, sullen head of Chelinda like a legendary blade, a crusader's jewelled sword, or the great Excalibur itself, held reverently in prayer against the lip and brow of the night. It made of the darkness a wayside altar, a chapel at which the undubbed soul might come for its final vigil and dedicate a sword to the quest for a single grail. It was itself a Sword-of-all-such-Swords; but also it was a cross held over a world old in time, but new in the European heart.

And what does that mean? What does any cross mean? These shapes of crosses litter our horizons from birth to the grave, but do we know what they mean? Out of what tender wood, by what great carpenter, are they nailed?

We must shut our eyes and turn them inwards, we must look far down into that split between night and day in ourselves until our head reels with the depth of it, and then we must ask: "How can I bridge this self? How cross from one side to the other?" If we then allow that question to become the desire for its own answer, and that desire to become a bridge across the chasm, then, and only then, from high above on this far peak of our conscious self, on this summit so far above the snow-line of time, in this cold, sharp, selected moment, clearly and distinctly we shall see a cross. A gulf bridged makes a cross; a split defeated is a cross.

A longing for wholeness presupposes a cross, at the foundations of our being, in the heart of our quivering, throbbing, tender, lovely, lovelorn flesh and blood, and we carry it with us wherever we journey on, on unto all the dimensions of space, time, unfulfilled love, and Being-to-be. That is sign enough.

After that the drum can cease from drumming, the beating and troubled heart have rest. In the midnight hour of the crashing darkness, on the other side of the night behind the cross of stars, noon is being born.

Our last morning in the low country broke clear and fine. Our bearers and askaris, who had drummed and danced themselves almost to a standstill, set about trying to get ready for our journey. But Michael and I kept them at their work with such pitiless determination that we made an early start and got away before seven.

(The heart had been drummed out of the village too.) No one saw us off except the Chief who came limping along painfully on a stick, complaining that the walk and climb up Nkawozya had been too much for him.

The track up Chelinda started immediately behind the village. It was very steep but we all had our climbing legs now and went up it with a will. Once I stopped and far below down in the plain I saw the scarlet beret, the young gallant headgear of our Mpoka Umfumo, a tiny point of red bobbing up and down in the sombre track of the valley on that long difficult walk back to Mwatangera. I would probably never see him again, but that beret and he were a part of me I could never forget, if only for their presence at that moment of release from the war on Charo.

That was the last familiar thing we saw. From there on we got deeper into country which was different from anything we had seen. At first our track was lined with Euphorbias Candelabra, a tree so-called because it holds up the arms of its branches as if they were sockets in which the candles of the day are put to burn. When we climbed out of their Byzantine presence we came into a place dominated by immense scarlet aloes which raised the sun like some Burgundian wine towards a madonna blue sky. They in their turn gave way to white and scarlet proteas; the proteas to heathers, pink, white and russet bell heathers, yellow and white everlastings, and purple lobelias.

At that stage we came to a new view at the top of the head of Chelinda. For all its proud lift it was a false head. The real summit lay farther back at the end of a long, steep grass slope.

A loud cry went up from the bearers when they saw this slope. I am afraid it was not a romantic cry for all it said was "Meat! Meat! Meat!" and it meant to convey that ahead of us there was something they would like shot.

Over the slope all kinds of antelope and buck and gazelle were getting up out of warm beds in the grass to have a look at us. They were obviously not accustomed to this kind of intrusion, and though they could not possibly approve of it, the fear they had of it was the general fear of the unknown and not specific to man. As we advanced towards them, they gave way and scattered until in time the whole skyline was broken by their lovely, keen heads and proud delicate necks. They looked much nearer than they were and I refused all entreaties to shoot, although, alas, we would have to shoot sooner or later for food.

I now took the lead with Harneck and we went ahead of the bearers so that I could be free to scout around. Michael came on with the main body, keeping as near as he could on a southerly bearing, which was not difficult. There were wide, well-trodden game tracks everywhere and they all ran south. I, still deep under the influence of my night on the crest, was thrilled to see how clearly and unerringly everything pointed south.

When we came to the place where the first antelope had stood up, its bed was still warm with the warmth of its body, and the grass spread like a magnetic field around where he had lain. Then I suddenly became aware of a familiar, purple glow in the grass, the murmur as it were of a dark purple tide ebbing through the gold of the grass. Irises, the proud, erect flowers of chivalry, were everywhere. We walked from there, I reckoned, through ten square miles of irises. When this heraldic field of gold and purple ended we came to an altitude in which the grass glowed with the orange, red, blue and gold of wild gladiolus. Most lovely of all, enormous, single, white delphiniums shone like stars on all the darker slopes. In the background on the horizon were those beautiful, antelope heads still staring down at us. It was like some fine ancient tapestry suddenly come alive.

At about noon we were right on the top. At last there was no doubt, we were on the true Nyika, high above the low malarial plains, above sleeping sickness, east coast fevers and the paralysing maladies and parasites of the low country. We were so high that the air smarted in our nostrils; it was so keen and cold that we promptly put on our pullovers. But we had reached the summit. There were no more peaks to conquer, no more heart-breaking climbs up one steep valley and the next. We were on a real plateau; far as our eyes could see stretched a gentle, rhythmically-rolling country of grass and flowers. Round the edges other peaks rose out of the shimmering plain, giving us a keen sense of our exalted world; but they were not our concern save as additional ornament to the immense African frame of our view. South I could see for about fifty miles, then my view was blocked by cloud. But in the whole of the distance between there was nothing but this free, gently rolling country.

I wish I could describe the effect that view had on me, but I will say little more than that it seemed to me miraculous. It was so unlike anything else. It was deep in the heart of Africa and filled with the animals of Africa, and yet it was covered with the grasses, the flowers and colours of Europe. Yet it was unlike any other colour I have ever seen: I expect, basically, it was a tawny gold, the gold of the leopard's rather than the lion's skin, but this gold was shot through with undertones of a deep blood red and a shadowy purple.

As I looked at it, I understood at once why I had felt below that there was a large, purple cat purring up there behind the clouds. It looked in its colours, its shape and its isolation, a contented, serene, and deeply fulfilled land. It seemed a place which, without human interference, had made its own contract with life, struck its own balance with necessity and nature. Beyond that I cannot go.

After tea Michael, Karramba and I, taking our rifles, walked about two miles down the gentle dale through which the Rukuru ran. It was about twenty minutes before sundown when, round a bend in the stream, we came to a large pool, blue into its deepest depths with the evening sky. On the slope above it was a big grey boulder. All round the pool the mud and earth were deeply cut with the tracks of game. We went up the slope and sat behind a rock and waited to see what we could see.

There was no wind any more. There was no cloud or mist in the sky. I have never known such stillness. The only sound was the sound of one's blood murmuring like a far sea in one's ears: and that serene land and its beauty, and the level golden sunlight seemed to have established such a close, delicate, tender communion with us that the murmur in my ears seemed also like a sound from without; it was like a breathing of the grasses, a rustle of the last shower of daylight, or the swish of the silk of evening across the purple slopes.

Suddenly Karramba touched my arm. We could hardly believe our eyes. A very big male leopard, bronze, his back charged with sunset gold, was walking along the slope above the pool on the far side about fifty yards away. He was walking as if he did not have a care or fear in the world, like an old gentleman with his hands behind his back, taking the evening air in his own private garden. When he was about twelve yards from the pool, he started walking around in circles examining the ground with great attention. Then he settled slowly into the grass, like a destroyer sinking into the sea, bow first, and suddenly disappeared from our view. It was rather uncanny. One minute he was magnificently there on the bare slope and the next he was gone from our view. But as if to confirm his presence, three black crows without a sound came and perched themselves on the summit of the slope above him. They seemed to be watching the place where he had vanished as closely as we were, tucking their dark heads deep into their midnight shoulders with solemn absorption.

We waited attentively. About five minutes passed: not a sound anywhere, except this remote music of all our being. I was lying with my ear close to the ground when I heard a new sound that made my heart beat faster: it was the drumming of hooves far away. It was a lovely, urgent, wild, barbaric sound. It was getting louder and coming straight for us. I caught a glimpse of Michael's face, shining with excitement. The drumming of the hooves came towards us from somewhere behind the far slope, like a great Pacific comber, like a charge of Napoleon's cavalry at Waterloo, and then out of the midst of this drumming, this surf of sound, there was thrown up like a call on a silver trumpet, or the voice of an emperor born to command, a loud, clear neigh. It was one of the most beautiful sounds I have ever heard, and it established itself in all my senses like the far silver fountain that I had once seen a great blue whale throw up on a South Atlantic horizon after a storm. Now, as the sun tinted the horizon, the wave of sound rose towering into the air and then crashed down on to the summit of the slope opposite us. A troop of about forty zebra, running as if they had never known walking, the rhythm of their speed moving in waves across their shining flanks, charged over the crest and made for the pool where the leopard lay.

I wondered how it was going to end. I could not believe a leopard would attack such a lusty group of zebra, although I have never seen a leopard behave quite as this one did, so frankly, so openly. At that very moment, the leader of the troop, with his mane streaming from him like the strands of the Mistral itself, stopped dead. At one minute he must have been going at thirty-five miles an hour, at the next he stopped without a slither in his tracks, two fountains of steam shooting out of dilated nostrils.

The rest of the group stopped with him. Had they seen the leopard or seen us? For about five minutes we saw a group of zebra, not fifty yards away, in earnest consultation. I saw Michael raise his gun and then put it down again. He had, I knew, to kill one zebra because it was his duty to examine them for parasites. I saw him take aim several times but always he put his gun down again.

Meanwhile the consultation went on, soundlessly and ceaselessly. Some invisible, some electric exchange of meaning was going on between those vivid creatures on the darkening slope. They looked so heraldic, like unicorns who had just had their horns pared. They had beautifully marked golden skins, with black blazonings. For five minutes they stood, their steaming heads close together, and then somewhere in the magnetic depths of themselves, their meaning fused and become one. They whirled swiftly round and charged straight back over the crest straight into the dying day and we did not see them again.

"I am sorry," Michael said to me, breathing hard: "I am sorry but I just could not shoot: they were beautiful."

"I am glad you didn't," I answered.

We got up and walked back, and as we rounded the bend saw that it was not the leopard that had scared the zebra but the smoke of our camp fires rising straight up into the still air like a palm blue with distance. The camp was just on two miles away, but even that was not far enough for the timid herd.

That night I had another dream. I record it for exactly the same reasons and on the same terms as the first one. I would add only that I dream often about animals. I have lived and been brought up in wild places and animals mean much to me. I dream particularly about horses and, in a way that I do not define clearly to myself, I am influenced by my dreams of horses. When they are thin, tired, thirsty, when I have to drag them along with me, I take it as a kind of warning; and when, as once in the war, I dreamt that I was actually carrying a horse of mine, I was really alarmed. This dream, too, was about a horse, but it was different. Here it is:

I dreamt I caught my horse in a field covered with irises. It was a large black horse with a white star in its forehead. It was called Diamond. It was a cross between a hunter and a carthorse; a fast and sturdy horse, a horse fit to carry a knight in full armour. It reminded me of my mare, Duchess, as described in Lilian Bowes-Lyon's lovely poems about her. I mounted Diamond squarely and we set off at a fast thundering pace across the purple folds of the Nyika. The wind and sunlight whistled through Diamond's mane. A feeling of strength and security came from the horse through the close grip of my knees on its back. I seemed as content as it is possible to be.

# Chapter Twenty-four

WITH this dream my journey in Africa really ends. It is true I spent another three weeks on that lovely plateau, but there is nothing new to say of it. Always it was there as I have described it, alone with itself, its grass, flowers, and animals, and no people except us. Every morning we rose early, shook the dew or frost off our tents and made our way until sunset across a new tract of our exalted land.

We spent two nights at the sombre pond or lake at Kaulime where the serpent is said to live. We did not see the serpent itself, in spite of the fears of our bearers, but I must record that I, Karramba and Harneck all three missed dead-easy shots at game hard by Kaulime, too easy really to be laughed away. When we came back our bearers shrugged their shoulders and the drummer said: "But Bwana, don't you know that there is a powerful Mankwala, mighty medicine in that pond?"

I realized how wise I had been not to shoot earlier on. The light was clearer than I had imagined. I paced the distance to where I had first shot at the buck. I had thought it was a hundred to a hundred and twenty yards. It was six hundred and fifty paces. And I tell this story against myself because it shows how pure and clear the air was over the Nyika, and how full, easy and generous its distances. I am not a bad shot, but it took me five days before I shot my first game.

Every day we saw that warm, electric flicker of flame of game moving in the distance—heraldic zebra, roan antelope with horns like Saracens' swords, and giant eland with purple coats and immaculate white dew-laundered socks. Every morning, even when one did not see them, one knew that the great bronze leopards of the Nyika, with their Assyrian profiles, sat by the edges of their Druid circles of wood sunning themselves and drying the dew off their whiskers; and every evening without fail the great African sun, as it went down far away in Rhodesia, left its light standing like an archangel on the horizon with wide outstretched wings gathering the world to its breast.

For about a fortnight we moved like this through un-inhabited country, and then came down one evening in the dark mist at Nchena-Chena.

But we were not finished yet. We had to go back into the vast Rumpi cleft of the Nyika, before we were finished.

One day Harneck and I did a thirty-two-mile trek. We went to the western edge of this new world and looked down immense precipices, and over a black valley for about a hundred miles of peak beyond peak stretching far into the blue Rhodesias. We came back and drank some water at the source of the great Rukuru river. We stalked some zebra but had to abandon our stalk because a lion on the same mission scared them as soon as we scared him; then, as the sun began to sink, we made for our camp.

At that moment I had my first and only difference of opinion with Harneck. Our camp was out of sight, indeed we had no idea where Michael had pitched it. Harneck, swearing he recognized Michael's foot-prints, wanted to follow one set of tracks, I another. It seemed most un-reasonable for me to be arguing with a native born and bred to tracking. But I had had my lesson on Mjanje. I preferred to be the cause of my own mistakes and I in-sisted on going my way. Half an hour later we came on to a rise and saw the camp, perfectly pitched on the banks of the young Rukuru.

Two nights later we camped for the last time by the magic pond, dark and tragically still under the night sky, and so full of reservations that the bearers could hardly bear to look at it.

From there we did, although I say it myself, a remarkable and praiseworthy journey into the immense and extremely difficult Rumpi valley. Our carriers were beyond praise. They did some terrible climbs, loaded to the full, through deep gorges along vast precipices without a man falling out, and a week later, at two o'clock in the afternoon, we climbed out of our last valley and looked down on the shimmering red roofs of the Mission at Livingstonia.

We camped that night on the road, and in the morning said good-bye to our bearers. It was the last good-bye and made me very sad. It is always like that with journeys. One is as sad at the end as at the beginning; the reward lies in between.

The bearers, too, looked depressed, and as they walked by us down the red, dusty road to their home, I thought their farewell was deeper than usual, that ancient greeting: "We see you, Bwana! We see you."

"Aye! I see you," I called back: "I see you. Hamba Gahle. Go in happiness."

Michael stopped, suddenly tapped a cigarette impatiently on his case, lit it, looked at me and said: "And you? What will you do now? Will you ever come back?"

I said I didn't quite know. For the moment my work was over. My instinct was to get back as soon as I could to take up my own personal life where the war had interrupted it ten years before. It seemed to me by far the most important thing in the world to do: to begin trying to give to myself the wholeness, the singleness that I so wanted life and the world to have. But who could tell, I might be back. Africa was deep in me, and in the past sooner or later it had always brought me back.

I did not say so to him, but the truth was that Africa was with me whether I came back or not. For years it had stood apart from me: a dark, unanswered, implacable question in my life. It was that no longer. I felt that I was not leaving it, but taking it with me. I might even be able to give some of it to Europe, to the Britain that had given me so much. For the sort of journey that Michael and I had just done never really ends. Where the body stops travelling, the spirit takes over the trek; but sometimes they work together and then one visits unknown, unexplored places. For me the greatest journey of all was on the move in Europe, and I wanted without delay to add what I had of singleness to it in order to help it on its difficult way.

I then had to leave Michael by the roadside with his servants already packing up. He was tired and looked thin and rather wan. For nearly a month he and I had walked and climbed from sunrise to sunset without a day's rest, and I knew he needed it. So I had volunteered to go to the Mission and telegraph for our cars.

The Mission was about eight miles away. It was a bright, sunny day and, after the Nyika, the two-thousand-foot climb up that hill was child's play to me. At the top I turned round to look back. But there was the old familiar cloud over the top of the plateau, hiding it utterly from view.

I walked as fast as I could to a little post office that was all of a tremble in the lakeside sun. A black postmaster gave me a telegraph form and a strange, attentive look. I caught a glimpse of my face in a small mirror. It was burnt black by the sun, but was the clear fresh colour that is never seen in the hot, malarial plains.

Quickly I wrote my telegrams. The little Morse machine started ticking busily before I was finished. Among other telegrams, I sent this: "All done and hastening home."

VILLA DES ÉLÉPHANTS, LA NARTELLE
*and* LA PONATIÈRE, ISÈRE, FRANCE